Honda

Honda Civic 1200—1973-1979
Honda Civic 1300, 1500—1980
Civic CVCC—1975-1979
Accord—1976-1980
Accord LX—1978-1980
Accord (four-door)—1979-1980
Prelude—1979-1980

Other titles from

Popular Mechanics MOTOR BOOKS

BASIC CAR CARE ILLUSTRATED
BODYWORK & PAINTING
TUNEUP & TROUBLESHOOTING
CAR CARE GUIDES:

Buick
Chevy
Chrysler/Plymouth/Dodge
Datsun
Ford/Mercury Compacts
Ford/Mercury Intermediate/Full Size
Oldsmobile
Pontiac
Toyota
Vega
VW Beetle
VW Rabbit
X-Body

Allen Bragdon, Editor-in-Chief
Jacquelyn Crete, Project Director
Michael Eastman, Art Editor
James Egnor, Writer
Jay J. Iorio, Production Associate
Jeff Mangiat, Illustrator
John B. Miller, Designer

The editors are grateful for the assistance
provided by Rocky Delpriore, Service Manager,
Plaza Honda, Brooklyn, NY, and Fred
Mackerodt, Honda Public Relations, NY, NY.

Published by Hearst Books
A Division of The Hearst Corporation
224 W. 57th Street
New York, NY 10019
Also publishers of

MOTOR Auto Repair Manual
MOTOR Imported Car Repair Manual
MOTOR Truck Repair Manual

The information herein has been compiled from
authoritative sources. While every effort is made
by the editors to attain accuracy, manufacturing
changes as well as typographical errors and
omissions may occur. The publisher and the
editors cannot be responsible nor do they
assume responsibility for such omissions, errors
or changes.

Manufactured in the United States of America
by The Hearst Corporation
New York, NY 10019

Library of Congress
Catalog Card No. 80-80769

Soft Cover ISBN No. 0-87851-927-0

Car Care Guide

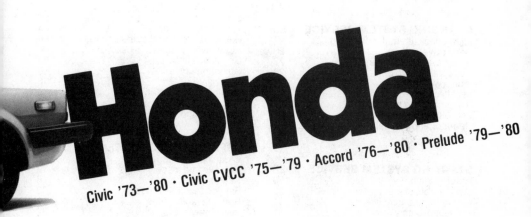

Civic '73—'80 · Civic CVCC '75—'79 · Accord '76—'80 · Prelude '79—'80

Contents

Foreword

This is a Honda Book

If you own a Honda—any Honda, of those models listed on page 1—this book is for you. It tells you—model by model, year by year—how to keep your car going longer and at lower cost. It won't be of much use to the owners of Chevettes or Miradas or Porsches. It was written by a Honda expert, illustrated with photos and drawings of new Hondas. It's a Honda book. Period.

When we, the editors, were assigned to this job by Popular Mechanics and *MOTOR* Manuals, we set out to produce a series of individualized Car Care Guides. We started by drawing up a master list of all repair and maintenance jobs that the do-it-yourselfer (even the first-time do-it-yourselfer) can handle. Then we matched that list with the peculiarities of each make and model. We looked for such factors as accessibility of components, ease of removal and installation, risk of damage or injury. Honda owners are fortunate in that the machine they drive is just right for the home mechanic.

Then we hired an expert on the Honda line who knows Hondas inside out. His job was to prepare step-by-step instructions in clear, simple language for each job the Honda owner can handle successfully in his or her home garage. After that, he guided our photographers and artists in gathering and preparing the 300 plus illustrations that demonstrate this "hands-on" technique step by step. Finally, when the people who lay out the pages and assemble the pieces had finished their work, our technical expert checked it before it went to the printer to make sure they had put the materials together correctly.

How to Use This Book

Chapters two through twelve, more than half this book, show how to perform each of the operations in a full engine tune-up. That's where the biggest payoff is in fuel economy and labor costs. *Maintenance* is the key to getting the best performance from your car. To *keep* your Honda tuned up you have to dip into the engine to make adjustments much more frequently than you must, say, install a new set of disc brakes. The first twelve chapters are arranged in the *order* you should work to perform an engine-maintenance tune-up. Each chapter covers a different operation. Each operation is described step-by-step.

The balance of the chapters show how to diagnose problems, and how to disassemble, replace, and reassemble components that can wear out or break in your Honda's suspension, brakes, and other systems. At the beginning of each chapter we provide a big exploded-view drawing that shows where all the parts are and what they are called. Further on you will find a box listing the tools you *must* have ready to do the job and other tools that are handy because they make the work easier, but are not essential. You won't need a whole garageful of tools and you probably already own many of those you absolutely must have. Generally, we have avoided the use of special tools. Jacks, lifting devices, and very heavy, bulky, and limited-use tools can often be obtained at local rental centers.

Check the "Pro Shop" tips scattered here and there throughout the book. These are short-cuts and professional hints that our editors picked up from the pros who do these jobs every day. We've also provided "Econotips" in most chapters. These fuel-saving tune-up and driving recommendations should help you save money on that ever more precious commodity, gas.

To find the page on which instructions for a particular repair job appear in this book, look in the Table of Contents in the front or in the Index in the back. The Appendix contains useful information on lubrication points, recommended service schedules, and tune-up specifications.

A note on safety: When you undertake a job, be sure to work slowly and carefully. We've printed *Cautions* about procedures which might be hazardous to your person in *italics*.
🛑 signs warn you of any steps which require special care to avoid damage to a part of your car.

You can start saving money by improving performance the moment you start putting this book to work on your Honda. It was made to be a working partner (even the glue in the spine is formulated to resist cracking when the book is laid open on the car fender). Good luck.

The Editors

1
Know Your Car

Your car is composed of a variety of systems, each with many operating parts. Through normal usage, many of the 15,000 or more parts in your car gradually deteriorate. Some parts wear out sooner than others because they work harder, while many can last the lifetime of the car.

The performance of each system, such as charging, starting, cooling, and brakes, depends not only on the condition of all its own parts, but also on the proper functioning of other related systems.

As systems begin to fail, your driving attitudes may change. Most drivers tend unconsciously to adjust their driving habits. When the brakes show signs of going soft, do you begin to pump them? Or, if the car is pulling to one side, are you correcting for it by steering differently? Keep in mind that you are dealing with a potentially hazardous condition that should be corrected by adjustments to the car, not by adjusting your driving habits. By familiarizing yourself with the basic systems that make your car run, you will be able to identify and correct many problems before they become costly and possibly dangerous.

To check and protect the systems in your Honda, you should follow certain periodic procedures. There are three separate (though related) aspects of car care: tuneup, maintenance, and troubleshooting.

Tuneup is a series of procedures that restore optimum performance, reduce exhaust emissions, and increase your gas mileage. You should tune up your Honda at regular intervals rather than waiting for a failure.

Maintenance is a series of procedures (sometimes including tuneup) that ensure that the various systems in your car operate as well, as safely, and as long as possible.

Troubleshooting is a procedure through which your car's ailments are diagnosed and tracked down. The symptoms are analyzed and the possible causes uncovered. Often the cure will require a tuneup, either because the out-of-tune parts were the cause of the problem or because the real cause can only be discovered after the car is properly tuned. Tuneup and

SHIFTER

DISC-BREAK ASSEMBLY

AXLE SHAFT

routine maintenance can help you avoid having to troubleshoot a problem. Also, if your car is routinely tuned and maintained, when a problem does occur a number of the possible causes will already have been eliminated.

But why are tuneup and maintenance important for a car that has been running well for a number of months without any evident problems? First, even though a car might sound and run fine, it is going through a continuous process of wear. Modern automobiles operate at high temperatures and friction is continually created, that is, the rubbing of metal against metal. Eventually all of the moving parts on a car wear out because of friction and heat. This is where tuneup and maintenance enter the picture. If a car is poorly maintained, some parts wear out after 30,000 or even 20,000 miles, while with proper maintenance the same parts might last for 100,000 or 150,000 miles.

A poor tuneup or dirty engine oil can cause

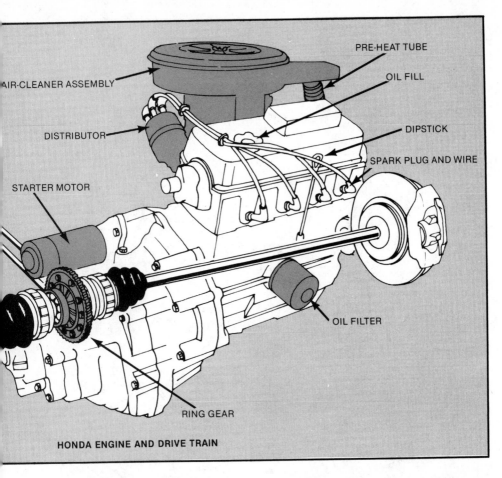

AIR-CLEANER ASSEMBLY

PRE-HEAT TUBE

OIL FILL

DISTRIBUTOR

DIPSTICK

SPARK PLUG AND WIRE

STARTER MOTOR

OIL FILTER

RING GEAR

HONDA ENGINE AND DRIVE TRAIN

major damage to the engine. Poorly maintained coolant or a loose fan belt may cause the engine to overheat. As a result, it may be necessary to rebuild or replace the entire engine, at a considerable cost. And the life of many systems on a car, such as brakes or suspension and steering, can be dramatically extended by simple and routine checks and adjustments. So a major reason for following regular tuneup and maintenance procedures is to increase the longevity of your car and therefore save money.

Tuneup and maintenance also ensure that your engine will operate at maximum capability and efficiency. An out-of-tune car will consume too much fuel and perform poorly. And at today's fuel prices, it is certainly worth it to spend the time and the cost of tuneup parts to get optimum gas mileage.

Finally, through routine maintenance you can usually avoid brake failure, tire blowouts, stall-

ing on a bridge or highway, overheating in crowded city traffic, and a host of other unexpected and potentially dangerous situations. Although how well your car runs and how long it lasts are undeniably important considerations, perhaps the most important is its reliability—how sure you can be that you will reach your destination safely.

If you have never worked on your own car, it may at first appear to be a very mysterious machine. All of those hoses, cans, tubes, and belts often cause beginners to throw up their hands and forget the idea of ever doing it themselves. But don't give up! With a little help you can figure out how most of the systems work and which ones you can work on. The first step is to introduce yourself to your Honda. Examine what's under the hood, look underneath the front and rear ends, and locate the major systems and parts. The drawings at the beginning of each of the following chapters will guide you in getting to know your car.

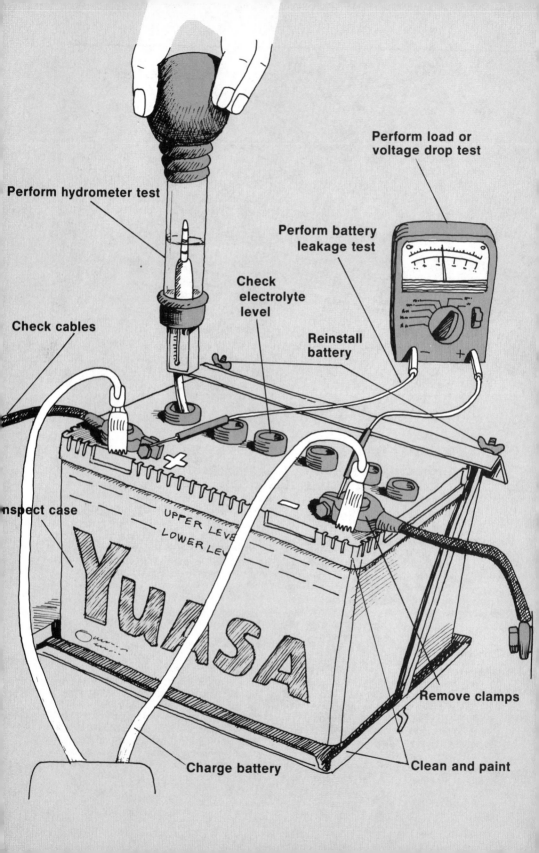

Perform load or voltage drop test

Perform hydrometer test

Perform battery leakage test

Check electrolyte level

Reinstall battery

Check cables

Inspect case

UPPER LEVEL
LOWER LEVEL

YUASA

Remove clamps

Charge battery

Clean and paint

2

Battery and Cable Service

1 Inspect case. Place a fender cover near the battery and inspect the case and top for cracks, leaks, bulges, warpage, and dirt (p. 12).

2 Perform battery leakage test. Testing the battery with a voltmeter will reveal whether a cracked case is causing it to discharge (p. 12).

3 Perform hydrometer test. This measures the specific gravity of the battery's electrolyte, but the test can only be performed on batteries of the non-maintenance-free type. A reading above 1.225 means the battery is OK for further testing, as long as the individual cell readings don't vary more than .030 points from each other (p. 13).

4 Check electrolyte level. Original-equipment Honda batteries have an almost clear case, so regular electrolyte inspection can be made at a glance. However, if in doubt, remove all cell caps to make sure all the plates are covered with electrolyte. For maintenance-free batteries, check the visual state-of-charge indicator if your Honda has one (p. 14).

5 Check cables. Inspect the cables for breaks and wear. Replace if necessary (p. 14).

6 Charge battery. Slow charging is the best way to renew life in a discharged battery (p. 15). Discharging may be caused by heavy use, neglect or a poor charge system.

7 Remove clamps. Remove the cable clamps from the battery posts. Inspect them and the terminals for deposits and corrosion. Clean, repair or replace as necessary (p. 15).

8 Clean and paint. Remove the hold-down clamps and lift out the battery with a lifting strap. Clean the case, top, clamps, and posts. Replace parts as needed. Clean the battery shelf (box) and hold-down clamps and paint with an acid-resistant paint (p. 16).

9 Reinstall battery. Return the battery to the case and reinstall the hold-down clamps and cables (p. 17).

10 Perform load or voltage drop test. To find out if your battery is putting out enough power to start the car under all conditions, perform a load or cranking voltage drop test with a voltmeter (p. 19). If the reading is above 9.5 volts (9 volts if performed below 0°C or 32°F), the battery is OK. If the reading is below 9.5 volts, charge the battery and retest. If the battery still fails the load or voltage drop test, you may have to replace it.

TOOLS

Essential. Basic tools • Goggles • Jumper cables • Jumper wire with alligator clips • Fender cover • Hydrometer • Wire brush •

Water (distilled or mineral-free) • Baking soda • Petroleum jelly • Towels or cleaning rags • Voltmeter • Terminal spreader • Acid-resistant paint.
Handy. Cable terminal puller • Battery post cleaning tool • Battery charger • Lifting strap • Battery pliers • Remote starter switch.

Inspect case

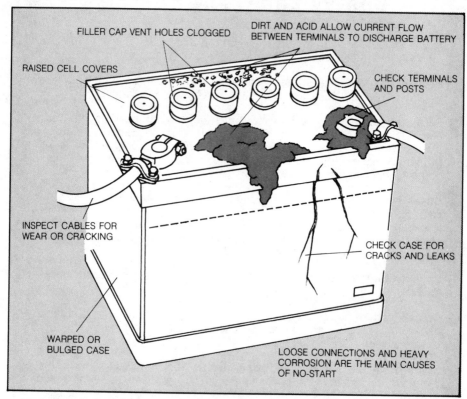

FILLER CAP VENT HOLES CLOGGED

DIRT AND ACID ALLOW CURRENT FLOW BETWEEN TERMINALS TO DISCHARGE BATTERY

RAISED CELL COVERS

CHECK TERMINALS AND POSTS

INSPECT CABLES FOR WEAR OR CRACKING

CHECK CASE FOR CRACKS AND LEAKS

WARPED OR BULGED CASE

LOOSE CONNECTIONS AND HEAVY CORROSION ARE THE MAIN CAUSES OF NO-START

1 Replace a battery which has cracks, leaks, raised cell covers, warpage or bulges.

2 Check for loose connections and heavy deposits of corrosion around the battery posts. This can cause a hard- or no-start condition. Tighten connections and clean to eliminate corrosion, if necessary.

3 Check, and if necessary clean, filler cap vent holes, terminals, and posts.

4 Inspect cables for wear or cracking and replace if necessary.

5 If the top of the battery is dirty or wet or has acid on it, clean it. Current flow between terminals can discharge a battery.

6 If wetness recurs after you have cleaned the top of the battery, there may be other problems, such as a hairline crack in the case or a faulty charging system.

Perform battery leakage test

Sometimes a battery will have such a slight hairline crack, you won't be able to notice it with the naked eye. If it goes undetected, it can cause the battery to run low on electrolyte and discharge.

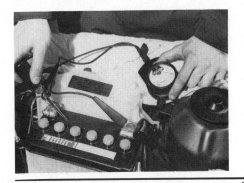

1 To check for this type of leakage, hook up a voltmeter to the battery. Attach the negative voltmeter terminal to the negative (−) post on the battery and the positive voltmeter lead to a screwdriver blade.

2 Move the screwdriver around the entire battery case, taking care not to touch the positive battery terminal. At the same time, watch the voltmeter needle. If the needle moves, it means the battery is discharging.

3 Clean the battery thoroughly and retest. If the voltmeter needle still moves, the battery has a crack and should be replaced.

Perform hydrometer test

1 Remove all caps from the battery cells.

2 Squeeze the hydrometer bulb, then insert the rubber hose into the first cell, keeping the hydrometer straight up.

3 Release the bulb and draw fluid into the tube until the float rises freely, then stop. Do not overfill the glass tube and do not remove the hydrometer from the battery.

4 Holding the hydrometer in a vertical position, note the specific gravity reading of the float. When reading the float, your eyes must be at the same level as the level of the electrolyte.

5 After writing down the specific gravity, squeeze the bulb and return the electrolyte back into the battery cell, then remove the hydrometer from the cell.

6 Repeat the above operation in all remaining cells. A fully charged battery should read between 1.260 and 1.280, a half-charged one should read 1.220, and a fully discharged battery will have a reading below 1.130. These figures depend on the temperature. All cells must be within .030 of each other. If they are not, and water has not recently been added, replace the battery. If the specific gravity is below specs, slow charge the battery. Remember, this can take many hours. Then retest with the hydrometer. If the battery fails the test again, replace it.

About hydrometers

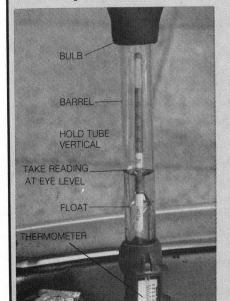

BULB

BARREL

HOLD TUBE
VERTICAL

TAKE READING
AT EYE LEVEL

FLOAT

THERMOMETER

A battery's acid and water mixture, called electrolyte, is checked with a hydrometer, which measures specific gravity (density or weight). But remember, maintenance-free batteries do not have removable cell caps, so you cannot perform this test on such batteries.

The tool consists of a glass tube with a rubber bulb on one end and a hose on the other. The electrolyte is drawn into the tube, and a calibrated float measures specific gravity. A good hydrometer compensates for variations in temperature and is inexpensive. Get the best and save yourself the trouble of correcting for temperature. However, if you must, add .004 points to your reading for each 10° above 80°F and subtract .004 points for each 10° below 80°F.

CAUTION: Electrolyte contains sulfuric acid, so wear protective clothing and goggles when working on a battery. If the electrolyte spills on your hands or face, wash it off immediately and thoroughly with water to prevent acid burn. If it spills on your clothing, wash it out at once or it will burn holes. Any electrolyte spilled on the battery, fender or engine parts must be washed off with water immediately to prevent damage. Rinse the hydrometer out with water when you have finished the test.

Check electrolyte level

Check the electrolyte level of your battery at least once a month. Regular electrolyte inspection on original equipment Honda batteries can be made at a glance, because they have an almost clear case. But, if in doubt, remove all the cell caps to make sure all plates are covered with electrolyte.

OR if your car is equipped with a maintenance-free battery that does not have removable cell caps, and the water level is low, the battery must be replaced. A sight glass on the top of some maintenance-free batteries lets you check the state-of-charge.

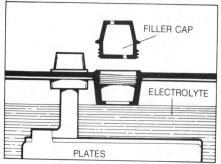

1 If the electrolyte level is low, fill each cell with distilled or mineral-free water only to the level of the split rings located in the bottom of the filler hole just above the plates.

2 Then slow charge the battery to mix the water and acid.

Check cables

Battery cables with high resistance because of wear, cracking, corrosion or looseness can be a major cause of a no-start condition. This condition may make you think your battery is at fault or even cause you to replace it needlessly. A careful inspection of cables and connections can save you time and maybe money.

1 When the insulation is cracked or frayed, the exposed wire encourages corrosion, which builds up resistance, eats away at the cable, and can cause hard starting. Damaged cables should be replaced.

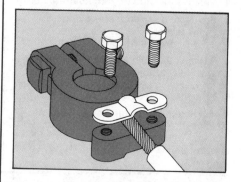

2 If only the terminal clamp is damaged, you don't have to replace the whole cable. Just cut off the clamp, strip off about ¾-inch of insulation, clean the cable thoroughly, and install a replacement clamp.

How not to blow up your battery

The battery in your car is a potential bomb. If you don't take the proper precautions, it could blow up in your face. The danger is greatest when you are using a charger, boosting a dead battery or boosting a frozen battery.

A battery always has hydrogen gases around the top. Any spark could ignite and explode this gas, so never smoke when working on a battery, and always ventilate the area around it. Remove all the vent caps and cover the openings with a damp cloth. This will act as a flame arrester and allow the gas to pass out.

Charging a battery

Switch on the charger only after all hookups have been made. Connect the positive clamp to the positive post first. Connect the negative clamp to a good ground at least a foot away from the battery. Make sure all electrically operated components are turned off. After charging, switch off the charger before disconnecting the clamps.

Boosting a battery

See the "Jump'er" box in this chapter for guidelines on how to hook up jumper cables correctly.

Charge battery

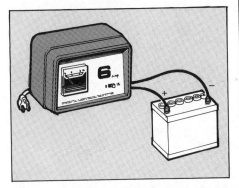

If your Honda battery is discharged but the electrolyte meets specs, the battery can be recharged. The best way to do this is with a trickle or slow-charge. There is less wear and tear on the battery and it will take a fuller charge. A slow-charge is ten percent of the battery's amp-hour rating. On a Honda, that's an average of 4.5 amps. A slow-charger of 4 or 6 amps is best. Keep in mind that for a severely discharged battery, it could take up to 24 hours to bring the specific gravity up to 1.250.

CAUTION: Never test or jump start an icy or frozen battery. Let it warm up to room temperature naturally.
CAUTION: Do not smoke while working over a battery, and make sure the area in which you are working is well-ventilated.

1 **To use a battery charger,** disconnect both cables from their posts, removing the negative cable first.

2 **Remove all filler caps,** then check and correct the electrolyte level in the battery.

3 **Connect the positive lead** of the battery charger to the positive (+) post of the battery and the negative lead to the negative (−) post. To operate the charger, refer to the instructions that came with it.

4 **Charge until the electrolyte's specific gravity** does not change on three consecutive hydrometer checks one hour apart. Don't let the battery temperature exceed 49°C (110°F). If your hydrometer is not the temperature-corrected type, don't forget to compensate for temperature.

5 **To avoid sparks,** unplug the charger before removing the clamps.

6 **Reinstall the filler caps** and connect both cables, positive cable first.

Remove clamps

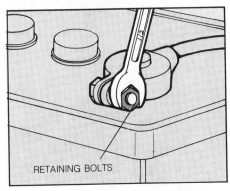

RETAINING BOLTS

1 **Loosen the cable retaining bolts** using a ten-millimeter combination wrench.

2 **Now remove the cable clamps** from the battery posts and inspect them and the terminals for deposits and corrosion.

3 **Clean, repair or replace clamps as necessary.**
STOP In more stubborn cases, you may have to use a terminal puller. Place the legs of the puller under the cable terminal and tighten the puller screw until the clamp comes off.

BATTERY CABLE TERMINAL REMOVER

STOP Always remove the negative (−) battery cable first, then the positive (+). When replacing the cables, install the positive first and the negative second. This will reduce the chance of sparks.

Clean and paint

1 **To remove the battery** from the box, always move the negative cable from the negative (−) post first, then remove the positive cable.

2 **Loosen the two ten-millimeter nuts** that hold the retaining bar on the top edge of the battery. You first may have to remove any rust with a wire brush and apply penetrating oil to the bolts.

3 **Use a lifting strap** to remove the battery—it's the safest and easiest way to do it. Note the position of the battery in the tray. On all Hondas, the negative post is closest to the front of the car.

4 **Set the battery on a solid surface** away from the car.

5 **Now mix a solution of baking soda and water.** To prevent the solution from getting into the cells, plug each cell cap vent hole with a toothpick (be careful not to break the toothpick in the cap). Then brush the mixture on the battery and in the battery box. Clean, then rinse thoroughly with clean water and wipe dry.

🛑 Even a small amount of baking soda will affect the battery's operation, so be very careful to plug the cell caps well.

6 **After cleaning the box** and the hold-down clamps, paint them with acid-resistant paint. This helps to retard corrosion.

7 **Clean the cable terminals** and battery posts with a special tool.

Reinstall battery

This procedure may be more easily completed if the windshield washer bag is temporarily removed from the retaining bar (on all models except Accords and Preludes).

1 Attach the battery strap to the clean or new battery and install it in the box with the negative (−) post closest to the front of the car. Don't forget the plastic tray insert under the battery if your Honda is so equipped. Reinstall the battery hold-down clamps and retaining bar.

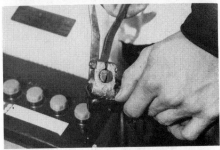

2 Always replace the positive cable to the positive post first, then the negative cable. With new clamps, new cables or a new battery, you may have to spread the clamps with a special spreading tool.

3 After tightening the terminal bolts with the proper wrench and making sure the terminals are tight on the battery posts, coat the terminals with petroleum jelly to retard corrosion.

ECONOTIP Changing rear-axle ratios to get better gas mileage certainly works. But the cost of the gear change is high and it will take a lot of driving to pay it off. So it isn't practical. But if you're buying a new car, selecting the right rear-axle ratio can make a lot of difference in the gas mileage you will get. When selecting a ratio, the higher the number, the faster the engine will turn, and the worse the gas mileage. For example, a 6-cylinder automatic transmission engine with a 2.71 rear axle will get two percent less mileage if a 2.94 ratio is used. Go to a 3.21 ratio, and the loss is seven percent. On a V-8 with an automatic transmission and a 2.45 ratio, the loss is six percent when going to a 2.71 ratio. Use a 2.94 ratio and the loss is 11 percent. It jumps to a whopping 17 percent when using a 3.21 ratio. All of these figures are for highway driving. The difference is much less in city driving, because the lower ratio helps only during steady cruising.

Jump'er

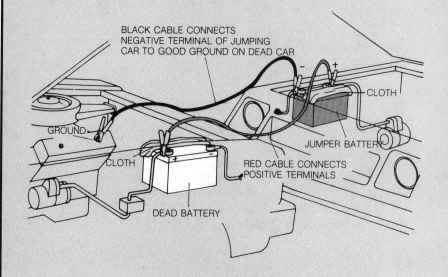

BLACK CABLE CONNECTS
NEGATIVE TERMINAL OF JUMPING
CAR TO GOOD GROUND ON DEAD CAR

CLOTH

GROUND

JUMPER BATTERY

CLOTH

RED CABLE CONNECTS
POSITIVE TERMINALS

DEAD BATTERY

The jumper cable is one of the most frequently used of all automotive accessory tools. Yet many people hook them up incorrectly and damage vital electrical components such as the battery or alternator.

When hooking up battery jumper cables, always trace the negative cable from the battery to its ground. This is the only way to determine which is the negative and which is the positive terminal. A red cable doesn't always mean positive. Be sure before you hook up the jumpers.

1 Connect the red jumper cable to the positive (+) terminal of the battery to be jumped and to the positive cable of the jumping car's battery.
2 Connective the negative (−) or black jumper cable to the negative cable of the jumping car.
3 Connect the other end of the negative jumper cable to a good ground, the alternator bracket or a heavy nut or bolt on the engine of the car to be jumped. Do not connect this end to the negative battery post or you may make a spark that could ignite the hydrogen gas around the top of the battery.
4 Start the engine of the car with the boosting battery and turn on the ignition of the car with the disabled battery.

5 When the disabled battery has been boosted, disconnect the cables, reversing the above order.

Jump-starting an engine with a battery from another car is a common procedure, but one which can be dangerous if precautions are not taken. Follow these rules for hooking up jumper cables:
• Open the hoods of both cars ahead of time to allow the hydrogen to disperse.
• Turn off your ignition and all electrical accessories to avoid draining power that might still be left in the battery.
• Put your transmission in Park (automatic) or Neutral (manual) and your parking brake on.
• Wear eye protection, gloves, and other protective clothing to guard against splashing acid.
• Remove all cell caps from the disabled battery and cover the openings completely with a damp cloth.
• Check the electrolyte level in the cells and add water, if necessary.
• Never jump a battery if the electrolyte is frozen. The battery could explode.
• Don't smoke or hold a flame near the battery.
• Make sure the two cars are not touching.
• Throw away all acid-soaked cloths.

Perform load or voltage drop test

The load or cranking voltage drop test checks the battery's capacity and its ability to deliver and hold the least amount of voltage needed to start your Honda under all conditions. Before proceeding with this test, make sure the battery is fully charged or has a minimum specific gravity of 1.225, temperature-corrected.

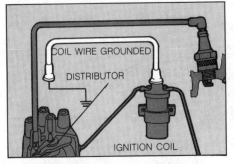

1 Unhook the high-voltage coil wire from the center tower of the distributor cap so the car won't start while you're cranking the engine. Then ground the coil wire.

2 To insure a good ground and lessen the possibility of spark, use a jumper wire with two alligator clips. Attach one end of the jumper to the free coil wire and the other end to a good ground

3 Connect the positive lead terminal of the voltmeter to the positive post of the battery and the negative lead terminal to the negative post.

4 If you do not have a helper to sit in the car and crank the engine, connect one lead of a remote control starter switch to the positive post on the battery and the other lead to the solenoid on the starter. On a Honda, this is the solenoid terminal with a female push-on connector that has a black wire with a white trace 🛑 On 1975 and 1976 CVCC's, there is a second black wire with a white trace, but this is held in place by a screw, not a push-on connector. Be sure you make your connection to the solenoid terminal.

5 Crank the engine for about 15 seconds and, at the same time, observe the voltage reading. It should not drop below 9.5 volts. If it does, the battery may have a leak or a defective cell.

6 To check, make sure the battery is fully charged by recharging on a slow charger. A slow 4 or 6 amp charger is more economical than a fast charger and will aid in the longevity of the battery.

7 Now retest the battery. If it still fails the test, you may have to replace it. But before you do, check the starting system. Note: A battery must always be charged after a load or voltage drop test.

Buying a battery

Let's say you're pretty sure you need a new battery, how do you decide which is the right one for your car? The big question you should ask yourself is: Will the battery deliver on the coldest morning? The amount of power a battery puts out on a zero-degree day is called cold-performance and it is that rating you should be looking at first when shopping for a battery. When the mercury dips to zero, a 60-month battery can shoot around 500 amps to your starter. An 18-month unit, on the other hand, will use only 240 amps.

How can you tell what your car's cold-cranking requirement is? Simple. Just take the engine's cubic-inch displacement figure and match it with the battery's cold-cranking rating. In cold climates, add 20 percent. For example: You live in Minnesota and drive a 1978 Honda Accord with a 1600 cc (98 cubic-inch) engine. You'll need a battery with a basic cold-cranking rating of about

100 amps. Therefore, in this case, buy a battery with a cold-cranking rating of not less than 120 amps.

Another rating that tells you about the battery's performance is reserve capacity. That number tells you how many minutes your car can keep running at night if your alternator dies on you. If a battery has a reserve capacity of 100, it means you can drive for 100 minutes on a balmy night without an alternator before the battery stops working altogether.

Battery warranties come in various forms. The most common offer an initial free replacement period of 90 days. After that, the rest of the warranty is broken down and prorated by months. If you buy a 36-month battery for $36.00, each month is worth $1.00. So if your battery fails in 24 months, you have $12.00 worth of credit toward another battery at the same store.

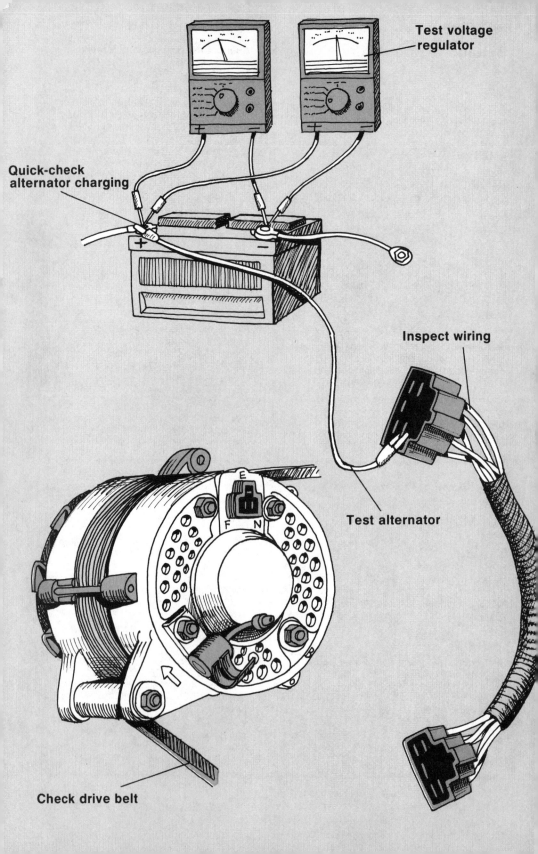

Test voltage regulator

Quick-check alternator charging

Inspect wiring

Test alternator

E

F N

Check drive belt

3

Charging System Service

PREP: Check the battery. Make sure it's fully charged (p. 11).

1 Quick-check alternator charging. First connect a voltmeter to the battery and note the voltage (p. 22). A battery in a good state of charge should read approximately 12.5 volts. Then start the engine. The voltmeter should now read close to charging voltage for your Honda, or between 13.5 and 14.5 volts. If the charging rate is outside of specs, shut the engine off and go to Step 2.

2 Check drive belt. Turn the alternator pulley by hand. If it moves easily, the belt is slipping and should be adjusted (p. 23). Repeat the test in Step 1.

3 Inspect wiring. Check the alternator and regulator wiring for looseness and corrosion. Make sure all the connections are clean and tight, and that the alternator and regulator are properly grounded (p. 24).

4 Test alternator. Disconnect the voltage regulator snap connector at the regulator and connect a jumper wire from the positive battery terminal to the white wire with a red trace. Run the engine at a fast idle and note the voltmeter reading (p. 25). If the amperage reading is within about ten percent of specs, then the alternator is OK and the regulator should be tested. If amperage is below specs, then further testing is necessary. Do not continue this test for more than 15 seconds or you may damage the alternator.

5 Test voltage regulator. Run the engine at a fast idle, 2000 to 2500 rpm, and note the voltage reading. If it is more than two volts higher than the battery voltage reading (see the reading in Step 1), and the alternator has been completely tested, the regulator is faulty and you should replace it (p. 27).

TOOLS

Essential. Basic tools • Jumper wire with male spade terminal and alligator clip •

Jumper wire with female spade terminal and alligator clip 36 inches long • Straightedge • Ruler • Voltmeter • Tachometer • Ammeter.
Handy. Fender cover • Drop light or flashlight • Belt tension gauge.

Quick-check alternator charging

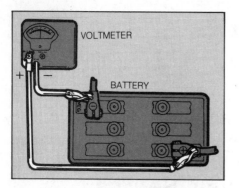

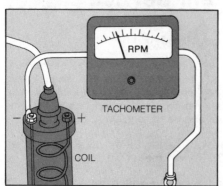

The charging system can give years of service with a minimal amount of maintenance. If system failure is suspected, prompt attention and repair may prevent damage to vital electrical components such as the alternator, regulator, battery, and even light bulbs and electrical wiring. If your alternator light or ammeter gauge, if you installed one, shows a low-charge, no-charge or discharge condition, perform this quick test to see if the problem is in the alternator or regulator.

1 First connect a voltmeter (in parallel) to the battery, with the positive lead going to the battery positive (+) terminal and the negative lead to the battery negative (−) terminal. Make a note of the battery's voltage. Note: A fully charged battery should read about 12.5 volts. If not within specifications, this may cause the alternator to malfunction. If necessary, charge and check the battery as described in the chapter on Battery and Cable Service. The battery must be fully charged in order to get a proper charging diagnosis.

2 Hook up a tachometer, connecting the positive (usually red) lead to the negative (−) terminal on the coil. Note: On your Honda there is a rubber boot covering the top of the coil. This can be turned inside out to get a better connection at the coil. Connect the negative (usually black) lead to a good ground.

3 Now start the engine and run it at a fast idle, about 1500 to 2000 rpm. Note the voltage reading and compare it with the battery voltage reading. The reading with the engine running and all electrical components off should be one to two volts higher than the battery voltage reading taken earlier.

4 With the engine still at a fast idle, turn on all electrical accessories. Battery voltage will drop. The reading should still be about one-half a volt higher than the battery voltage when the voltmeter was first hooked up. If either of these conditions is not met or the voltage goes higher than specs, you should thoroughly check the charging system. If within specs, the alternator and regulator are probably OK, but perform the regulator test as a further check.

Check drive belt

The component in the charging system most susceptible to failure is the drive (alternator) belt. This belt must be adjusted to the correct tightness or torque. If it's too loose, your battery may not charge and it will not start the engine. On your Honda, if the belt is too tight, it can damage the alternator or water pump bearings, since they are both driven by the same belt. This is a particular danger on the CVCC engine in which these units are opposite each other. Belts will usually tell you they're too loose by a loud squealing noise. A loose drive belt usually makes this kind of noise when a cold engine is started or when the car is suddenly accelerated.

1 To check the drive belt for looseness, turn the alternator pulley by hand. If it moves easily, the belt is probably slipping. If so, inspect it carefully, especially for glazing.

2 Inspect the underside of belts by twisting them. If they are cracked, cut, frayed, glazed or covered with grease, you should replace them.

3 To check drive belt tension, place a belt tension gauge halfway between the alternator pulley on both the CVCC and Civic 1200 engines. This will be more difficult on Hondas that have air conditioning. Instructions for the use of the gauge will usually be found on the tool itself.

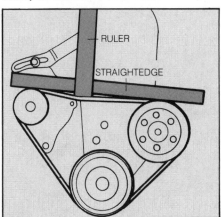

OR if you don't have a belt tension gauge, you can check belt tightness with a straightedge and a ruler. Bridge the alternator and water pump pulleys with the straightedge. Press down with about 20 pounds of pressure on the belt halfway between the two pulleys with the edge of the ruler. If the belt sags more than five-eighths of an inch, it is too loose.

To adjust drive belt tension

Drive belts are usually adjusted by moving the part that is driven by the particular belt. However, the alternator and water pump share the same belt.

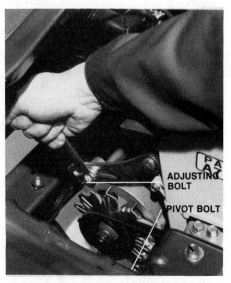

1 Locate and loosen the adjusting lock bolt on the alternator. The adjusting bolt is usually found in a slotted bracket.

2 Loosen the pivot bolt. This bolt is at the bottom of the alternator on the front and has a nut on the back.

3 To tighten an alternator belt, hold the alternator in a taut position with a pry bar and carefully pry against the alternator case and the engine block.
🛑 When you want to move a part with a pry bar, be careful where you position the bar, especially on a Honda with air conditioning and power steering. Do not lean the bar against the alternator fins, and make sure the bar is well-positioned so it does not slip and scrape your knuckles.

4 Check the belt's tension and when it's correct, tighten the alternator's adjusting bolt and the pivot bolt. Then recheck.

To replace drive belts

Other belts in the engine compartment, air conditioning, power steering, and air-injection belts, are checked in the same manner as described previously. These belts should all be checked periodically and replaced when necessary.

1 To replace any belt, move its accessory toward the engine and slip the belt over the pulleys. To replace a belt near the engine, you must first remove any other belts in front of it.

2 Loop the new belt over the crankshaft pulley, then over the accessory pulley.

3 Check alignment to make sure the belt is in the right place.

4 Finally, adjust belt tension and make sure all nuts and bolts are tightened.

PRO SHOP When new drive belts are first installed, they are stiff and may loosen after a short break-in period. You should recheck the tension of a newly installed belt after about 100 miles of driving.

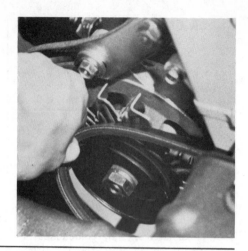

Inspect wiring

On Accords, Preludes, and 1980 Civics, the alternator and regulator harness is entirely within the engine compartment. This harness, starting at the battery and regulator, goes up the right side towards the firewall, then across and down the left side to the alternator, which is between the engine and the front of the car.

OR if you have a 1975–79 CVCC sedan or wagon, like the Accord the harness starts at the battery and regulator and goes up the right side. But, on these models, the wire harness goes through the firewall and into the passenger compartment and to the fuse box, then across the car inside and under the dash and out through the firewall on the left side and down to the alternator and back again.

OR if you have a 1973–79 Civic 1200, it almost identical to the CVCC sedan models in that the harness goes through the firewall and into the passenger compartment before reentering the engine compartment. On these Civic models, unlike the CVCC models, the alternator is on the firewall side of the engine. So the alternator wire harness on the Civic models is shorter than on the CVCC's.

Note: The 1975–79 CVCC sedans and wagons and the 1973–79 Civic 1200's are similar in that they have part of the alternator and regulator harness going inside the car. So a loose connection is possible inside the passenger compartment.

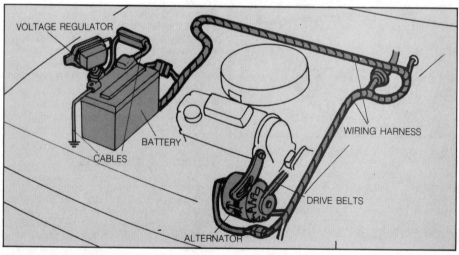

1 Check all connections at the alternator, the voltage regulator, and the wiring harnesses for looseness and corrosion.

2 Make sure the alternator and the regulator are grounded properly.

3 Check wires for cracks, breaks or fraying. Frayed wires may accidentally ground, causing the charging system to short out or to work overtime.

4 Make sure the alternator mounting bolts are tight and properly grounded.

5 Don't forget to check the main fuse(s) and fuse box for blown fuses.

🛑 The wiring harness for the alternator on the CVCC engine connects to the left-hand engine compartment harness at a point low and between the left wheel well and the front of the alternator. This snap connector, as well as others in the engine compartment, should be inspected and cleaned of any corrosion. Then on the wire sides of the connectors, pack with a silicone grease to retard corrosion.

Test alternator

1 Connect a voltmeter and tachometer as shown for quick-check alternator charging.

AMMETER

2 Also connect an ammeter. Follow the instructions that come with the instrument. 🛑 Before beginning the test, make sure the battery is fully charged, the alternator belt is properly tensioned, and everything electrical is turned off.

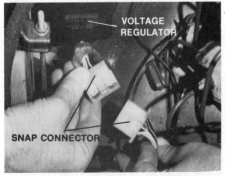

VOLTAGE REGULATOR

SNAP CONNECTOR

3 Disconnect the six-pin (only five wires) voltage-regulator snap connector at the regulator.

WIRE HARNESS CONNECTOR

JUMPER WIRE

4 Full field the alternator by using a special jumper wire with a male spade terminal on one end and an alligator clip on the other end. First, to prevent sparks, connect the male spade terminal end of the jumper wire to the field wire (the white wire with a red trace) in the wire-harness connector that connects to the reglator.

5 Now connect the alligator clip end of the jumper wire to the positive cable of the battery.

6 Start the engine and operate it at a fast idle, 2000 to 2500 rpm. The ammeter will show the total amperage output of your alternator and that reading should be within five amps of the specifications listed on the chart.
CAUTION: Do not operate the alternator under this condition longer than 15 seconds because it is now running unregulated and could overcharge the battery.

MAIN FUSE
1980 ACCORD
BATTERY

7 If the amperage reading is below specifications, check the main fuse, which is located near the battery.

Note: On CVCC, Accord, and Prelude models, the alternator is located between the engine and the front of the car.

OR if you have a Civic 1200, the alternator will be more difficult to hook up because it is on the firewall side of the engine and under the distributor.

8 If the main fuse is OK, with the engine off disconnect the FEN plug.

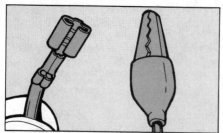

9 Use a special jumper wire, this one approximately 36-inches long with a female spade terminal on one end and an alligator clip on the other end. First, to prevent sparks, connect the female spade terminal to the back of the alternator on the F terminal. Now, connect the alligator clip end of the jumper wire to the positive terminal of the battery.

10 Start the engine and again operate for no longer than 15 seconds at a fast idle.

11 If the amperage reading is still below specifications, replace the alternator. **STOP** If you replace the alternator, quick check the new one.

12 Thoroughly check all snap connectors and wires between the alternator and the regulator and then check the regulator.

13 After all alternator testing has been completed, shut off the engine and make sure all jumper wires are removed and all snap connectors are reinstalled.

14 Don't remove the ammeter, voltmeter or tachometer. They will be used next to test the voltage regulator.

To replace the alternator

If the tests indicate that your alternator is not putting out enough power to the battery and the car's electrical system, you should replace the alternator.

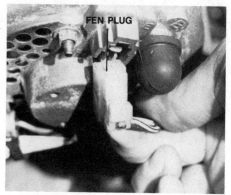

FEN PLUG

1 Disconnect the battery's negative cable, then remove the FEN plug connector at the back of the alternator and the battery wire from its terminal at the rear of the alternator.

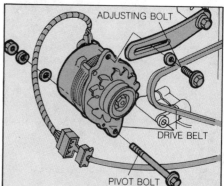

ADJUSTING BOLT

DRIVE BELT

PIVOT BOLT

2 Now loosen the adjusting bolt and the pivot bolt.

3 Push the alternator toward the engine to free the drive belt from the alternator pulley.

4 Remove the belt from the alternator, then the bolts and the alternator itself from the engine.

5 Reverse this procedure to install the replacement alternator.

6 Adjust the drive belt tension and reconnect all the electrical wires, then reconnect the negative battery cable.

7 Start the engine and test the alternator's output again.

Test voltage regulator

On some Honda models, the Civic 1200 for example, the voltage regulator is attached to the fender well beneath the main fuse box.

Before attempting to test the voltage regulator, all lights and accessories must be off and the battery fully charged. You should have recently tested the alternator system to make sure it is working properly. If it is not, you may get a false regulator diagnosis.

1 With the ammeter, voltmeter, and tachometer still hooked up from the alternator test, start the engine and let it operate at a fast idle of approximately 2000 rpm. The amperage reading on the ammeter should read less than ten amps. If the reading is more, you must charge the battery before the regulator test can be completed.

2 When you have an amperage reading of less than ten amps, note the voltage reading, which should be between 13.5 and 14.5 volts. If the voltage reading is outside of these specs and the alternator tested OK, replace the voltage regulator.

🛑 An open in any of the wires in the charging system may result in conditions ranging from overcharging to no charge at all.

🛑 Use caution when replacing the regulator because you are working near the battery.

3 To replace the voltage regulator, first check its location. On all models except the Accord, it is on the inner fender well behind the battery. If you have a Civic 1200 or a CVCC sedan or wagon produced before 1980, you may first have to remove the battery to gain proper and safe access to the voltage regulator. If you have to remove the battery in order to remove the voltage regulator, follow the removal and safety procedures outlined in the chapter on Battery and Cable Service.

OR if you have an Accord, the voltage regulator is located to the side of the battery.

4 Disconnect the snap connector. Most Honda regulators have a locking clip that must be pushed down to release the plug connector to the regulator.

5 Remove the two ten-millimeter regulator-retaining bolts with the proper tools.

6 Then install the replacement regulator, tighten the retaining bolts securely, and reconnect the snap connector.

7 Retest the charging system to make sure everything is working properly.

ALTERNATOR AND REGULATOR SPECIFICATIONS

Model	Year	Amp Rating	Regulated Voltage
Civic 1200	1973	35	13.5–14.5
	1974–1977	40	13.5–14.5
	1978–1979	45	13.5–14.5
Civic CVCC	1975–1979 with A/C	35	13.5–14.5
		45	13.5–14.5
Accords	1976–1980	50	13.5–14.5
Prelude	1979–1980	50	13.5–14.5
Civic (CVCC)	1980	45	13.5–14.5

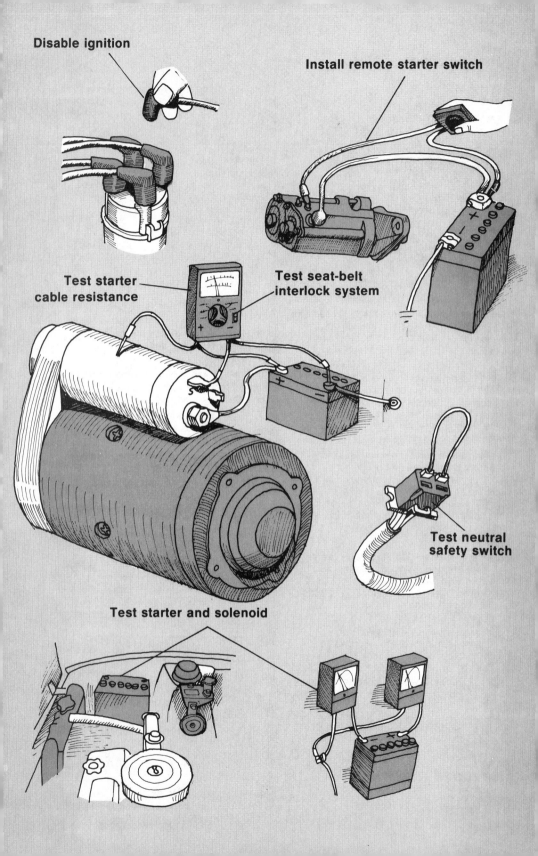

Disable ignition

Install remote starter switch

Test starter cable resistance

Test seat-belt interlock system

Test neutral safety switch

Test starter and solenoid

4
Starting System Service

PREP: Make sure the battery is in a good state of charge, all lights and accessories are turned off, and the cables are tight and free of corrosion (p. 10). Put the transmission in Neutral (manual) or Park (Hondamatic), then set the parking brake.

1 **Disable ignition.** To prevent the engine from starting during the test, remove the coil wire from the center of the distributor cap and ground it with a jumper wire (p. 30).

2 **Install remote starter switch.** If you don't have a helper to crank the engine from inside the car, you'll need a remote starter switch (p. 30).

3 **Test starter cable resistance.** Use a voltmeter calibrated in tenths of a volt (p. 31).

4 **Test neutral safety switch.** On Hondas, this switch is often referred to as the inhibitor/back-up light switch assembly. If the engine doesn't crank in either Neutral or Park, it may be due to a faulty neutral safety switch. To test, you'll have to bypass it. If the engine starts in any drive gear or in Reverse, the neutral safety switch should be repaired or replaced immediately (p. 31).

5 **Test seat-belt interlock system.** This system is found in 1974 and early 1975 Hondas and could be the cause of a no-start condition (p. 33). The average do-it-yourselfer could bypass the interlock system for testing purposes, but for testing of other components, it may be necessary to have the interlock system examined by a professional mechanic.

6 **Test starter and solenoid.** The 1973–80 Hondas, because of the integral design of the starter and solenoid, can best be tested as a single unit. With a voltmeter, ammeter, and tachometer hookup, you can check for starter engagement, wear or damage, cranking voltage and current draw, and cranking rpm and starter disengagement (p. 34).

Essential. Basic tools • Jumper wire •
Ammeter • Voltmeter • Ohmmeter • Test
light • Wheel chocks.
Handy. Droplight or flashlight • Fender
cover • Wire brush or sandpaper • Remote
starter switch.

Disable ignition

This is a safety measure to make sure the
engine doesn't start during the test.

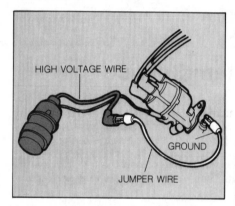

HIGH VOLTAGE WIRE

GROUND

JUMPER WIRE

**1 Remove the ignition coil secondary
wire** at the distributor cap. This is the wire
that leads from the coil to the center of the
cap.

2 Ground this wire. For a surer ground, use
a jumper wire with alligator clips at both
ends.
🛑 Never remove the wire from the coil's high
tension tower because the spark arcing to the
coil primary side could ruin the coil. Note:
The 1979 Accords and Preludes and all 1980
Hondas have transistor ignitions, not high
energy ignitions, and may be disabled in the
same manner.

Install remote starter switch

Since you'll want to observe the starting system
components as you test them, it would be an
advantage to install a remote starter switch.
This will enable you to crank the engine from
under the hood if you don't have a helper to sit
in the car and crank it.

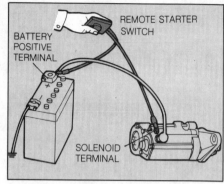

REMOTE STARTER
SWITCH
BATTERY
POSITIVE
TERMINAL

SOLENOID
TERMINAL

**1 Connect one lead of the remote starter
switch** to the smaller solenoid terminal (it
has a black wire with a white trace).

🛑 On 1975 and 1976 CVCC's, and some
California Civics, there may be a second
terminal having a small black wire with a
white trace. However, this wire is held in
place with a small screw. It is not the
terminal to use with your remote starter
switch.

2 Connect the other lead from the remote
starter switch to the positive (+) terminal on
the battery.

🛑 With the remote starter switch connected,
the engine can be started in any gear. So
make sure the emergency brake is set and
the transmission is in Neutral (manual) or
Park (Hondamatic).

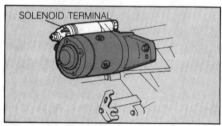

SOLENOID TERMINAL

**Civic models from 1973–79 and some of
the 1980 Civics,** California models, utilize a
starter similar to this one. The remote starter
switch is hooked up in the same manner as
on the CVCC's. That is, one of the leads is
connected to the solenoid terminal having the
black wire with a white trace with a female
terminal spade connector. The other lead of
the remote switch is connected to the
positive (+) terminal on the battery.
    Like the 1975 and 1976 CVCC models,
some of the 1980 California model Civic's
also have a second black wire with a white
trace, and it too is connected to the solenoid
with a small screw and is not the terminal to
be used for the remote starter switch.

Test starter cable resistance

Slow cranking or hard starting can be caused by battery cables that are damaged or under-sized, by loose terminals or by corrosion. One method of measuring starter cable resistance is to test voltage drop in an insulated circuit, such as from the battery to the starter. To test the starter cables for resistance, you'll need a voltmeter calibrated in tenths of a volt.

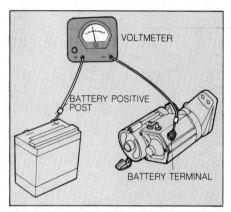

1 **Hook up the voltmeter positive lead** to the positive battery post. Connect the negative voltmeter lead to the battery terminal of the starter.

2 **Disable the ignition** and crank the engine. The voltmeter reading should read less than 0.2 volts. If it is higher, and the connections are tight, replace the cable.

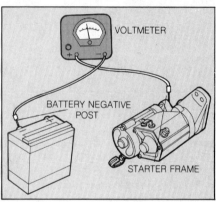

3 **To check the ground circuit resistance,** connect the voltmeter negative lead to the negative battery post and the positive lead to the starter motor frame. Again, with the ignition disabled and the engine cranking, a voltage reading higher than 0.2 volts indicates a poor ground circuit. This may be caused by a poor ground wire or connection or even a loose starter mounting.

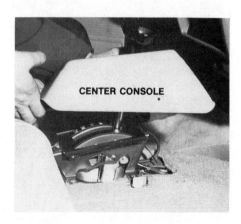

Test neutral safety switch

On all Hondamatics, the neutral safety switch (inhibitor/back-up light switch) is located in the center console attached to the shifter assembly. On 1973–79 Hondas, the swith is on the passenger side. For access to the switch, remove the center console. On most models there are four attaching screws, two in front on each side and two at the very back of the console.

1 To test this type of switch, on all Hondamatics except 1979 and 1980 Accords and Preludes, unplug the snap connector leading to the neutral safety switch.

2 Using the wire harness with the four-prong female-type connector, not the connector going to the neutral safety switch, connect a jumper wire between the two black wires with a white trace. You have now bypassed the neutral safety switch. *CAUTION: With this jumper wire connected, the engine can be started in any gear, which could cause the car to lunge forward or backward. Be sure the emergency brake is set and the transmission is in Park.*

3 Turn the ignition to the start position. If the starter now cranks the engine, the neutral safety switch is defective and must be replaced.

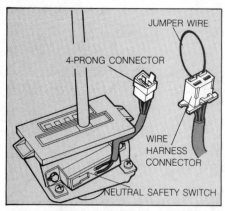

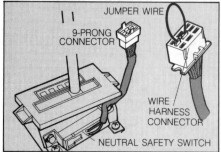

OR if you own a 1979 or 1980 Accord or a 1980 Prelude with Hondamatic transmission, it has a nine-prong connector. However, the test is the same. Locate and jump the two black wires with a white trace that are found in the female connector of the wire harness. Again, if the engine now cranks, the switch is defective and must be replaced.

To replace the neutral safety switch

1 To replace the neutral safety switch, unplug the snap connector. On older models also unplug the blue and yellow wires that go toward the back.

2 Remove the two attaching bolts and the switch.

3 To install the new neutral safety switch, make sure the actuator sticking out of the lower end of the selector lever and the slot inside the slider part of the switch line up.

4 Then line up the mounting bolts and secure the neutral safety switch to the shift mechanism.

5 Now set the emergency brake and make sure that the car starts only when the selector lever is in Park or Neutral. If not, adjust according to the procedures which follow. On all Hondamatics, as a double check on the switch, turn the ignition switch on and put the selector in reverse. With the emergency brake set, make sure the backup lights are working.

6 Reinstall and secure the console.

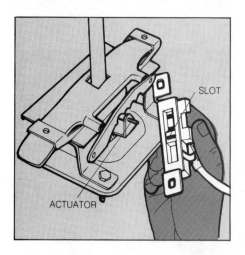

To adjust the neutral safety switch

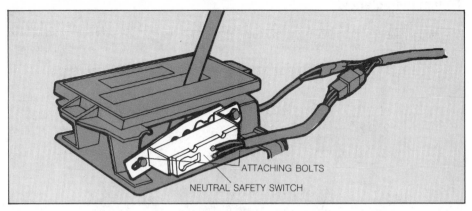

ATTACHING BOLTS

NEUTRAL SAFETY SWITCH

There are a few cases when the neutral safety switch may simply be out of adjustment, causing a no-start condition or starting in Drive or Reverse. This may be caused by loose attaching screws or excessively hard use of the shifter mechanism. To check for possible maladjustment, loosen the two neutral safety switch attaching bolts, slide the switch forward, and retighten the bolts. With the selector lever in Neutral or Park, but not in Drive or Reverse, the engine should start. If the starter does not crank the engine when the transmission is in Park, loosen the two attaching bolts again and slide the switch backwards, then recheck. Readjust the switch if it does not function correctly. If you cannot adjust it properly, it must be replaced.

Test seat-belt interlock system

If you own a 1974 or 1975 Honda, a no-start condition can be caused by a faulty seat-belt interlock system. This system was required in 1974 by Federal Motor Vehicle Standards. So if you own one of these models, it will have an interlock system that controls current flow from the starter solenoid, which in turn activates the starter. This system requires the driver and/or passenger to have their seat belts buckled before the car will start. The system is complex. The average do-it-yourselfer can perform only a bypass test to either condone or condemn the system. Extensive testing of the system and its components requires the services of a professional mechanic.

1 If a no-start condition exists and the seat-belt interlock system is suspected, first locate the emergency start switch on the right shock tower and use it to try to start the engine. If a no-start situation still exists, use a voltmeter for further testing.

2 Connect the negative voltmeter lead to a good ground and the positive lead to the starter solenoid terminal (the small terminal with a female spade connector and a black wire with a white trace).

3 Turn the ignition switch on and engage the emergency start switch, then note the voltmeter reading. If there is a voltage reading, then the interlock system is OK and you will have to test the starter and solenoid. If there is no reading on the voltmeter and the starter tests OK, then the interlock system is faulty and should be further tested by a professional mechanic.

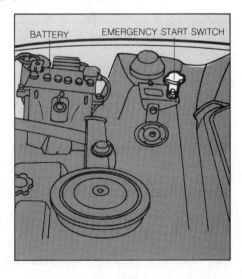

BATTERY   EMERGENCY START SWITCH

Test starter and solenoid
To test the solenoid

The integral starter-and-solenoid system used on CVCC's, with a gear reduction starter, will be generally discussed as a unit. However, this is a quick test for the starter solenoid alone. The Civic starter and solenoid are less integrated and the solenoid is very easily tested.

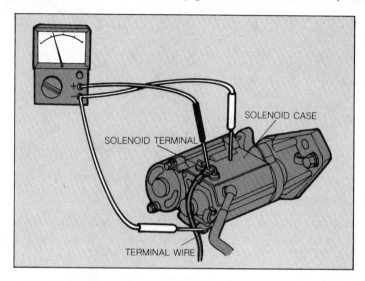

SOLENOID CASE

SOLENOID TERMINAL

TERMINAL WIRE

1 Connect one lead of an ohmmeter to the small solenoid terminal (the terminal with the small black wire with a white trace). Connect the other ohmmeter lead to the solenoid case. There should be no reading on the ohmmeter.

2 Move the ohmmeter lead from the solenoid case to the terminal wire between the solenoid and starter. Now the ohmmeter should have a reading. If both these tests checked out, then the solenoid is OK. But, if either test failed, the solenoid is bad and should be replaced.

STOP On most Honda models, the solenoid can only be removed by disassembling the starter, so it is best left to a professional mechanic.

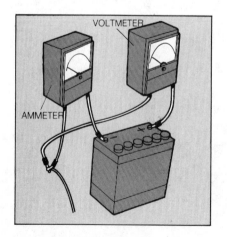

VOLTMETER

AMMETER

To test the starter

To test the starter, the engine should be warmed up, at least 38°C (100°F) and the battery and cables should be in good condition.

1 First disable the ignition so the engine does not start, and for convenience install a remote starter switch.

2 Then connect an ammeter to the battery, following the instructions on the instrument.

3 Next connect a voltmeter in parallel to the battery, that is positive lead to positive battery terminal and negative lead to negative battery terminal.

4 Connect a tachometer to the distributor, usually the red lead to the negative (−) terminal on the distributor and the black lead to a good ground.

🛑 Anytime you are working on a car, there is danger of its lunging forward or backward. This is especially true when testing the starting system. So chock the wheels securely to keep the car from moving.

5 Put the transmission in Park (Hondamatic) or Neutral (manual), and engage the emergency brake.

6 Crank the engine, either from the ignition switch or remote starter switch, noting and writing down as quickly as possible the readings on the ammeter, voltmeter, and tachometer. Using the ignition switch or the remote starter switch, the starter should engage and produce a smooth and steady cranking of the engine.

🛑 Do not operate the starter for more than 30 seconds at a time, and always allow the motor to cool off for at least two minutes before cranking again. Continuous cranking can cause overheating and damage to the starting motor.

7 If the engine does not start with the ignition switch, try using the remote starting switch or a jumper wire from the battery positive terminal to the solenoid terminal that has the black wire with a white trace, but be careful of sparks.

8 A good amperage reading on the ammeter would be between 130 and 180 on all 1973–80 Hondas. Some of the newer model 1980 Hondas have a maximum allowable amperage draw of 230 amps. However, the closer to the 160 or 180 amp reading the better and the longer the whole starting system will last. Compare your voltage reading with specifications. During engine cranking, the voltmeter reading should not have dropped below 9.5 volts. An exception would be some of the newer models with a higher allowable amperage draw. The voltage in this case should not drop below 8.5 volts.

9 Next, check engine cranking rpm. The tachometer should have read approximately 300 to 400 rpm during the cranking test.

10 Turn the ignition switch to the start position as a further test, then release the switch to the run position, noting the starter drive gear engagement and disengagement from the flywheel. The disengagement should be smooth and immediate with no hanging up. If not, the starter should be replaced.

Starts and stops

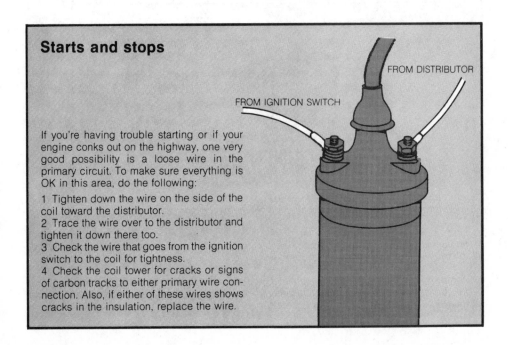

FROM DISTRIBUTOR

FROM IGNITION SWITCH

If you're having trouble starting or if your engine conks out on the highway, one very good possibility is a loose wire in the primary circuit. To make sure everything is OK in this area, do the following:

1 Tighten down the wire on the side of the coil toward the distributor.
2 Trace the wire over to the distributor and tighten it down there too.
3 Check the wire that goes from the ignition switch to the coil for tightness.
4 Check the coil tower for cracks or signs of carbon tracks to either primary wire connection. Also, if either of these wires shows cracks in the insulation, replace the wire.

To remove the starter

1 Disconnect the negative battery cable from the post and then the positive cable.

2 Now disconnect the starter solenoid wire by simply pulling it off.

3 Remove the starter cable from the starter. On models with the second black wire with a white trace, remove the small screw (be careful not to lose it).

4 Remove the two mounting bolts.

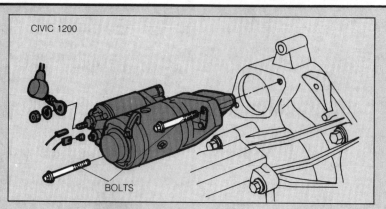

CIVIC 1200

BOLTS

Civic 1200 models from 1973–79 and the California CVCC models from 1977–80 have two long bolts going through the starter from the same side. The bolt on the top is threaded into the engine.

There are two holes in the starter, only one of which is used. Usually it's the upper one on manual transmissions and the lower for Hondamatics. Be sure to mark the hole before removing the bolt.

On these models, the lower starter bolt is difficult to see and is secured by a nut on the engine side so you may have to use two wrenches.

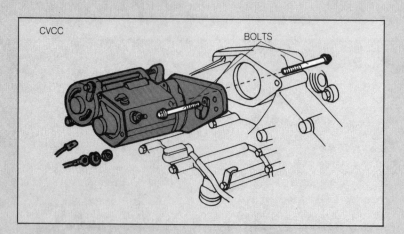

CVCC

BOLTS

On most of the CVCC models from 1975–80, including Accords and Preludes, there are two long bolts going through and securing the starter from opposite directions. Again, the upper starter bolt is threaded into the engine. Note that this starter also has two upper holes. Mark the one being used. On these models, the lower starter mounting bolt is threaded into the starter from the engine side and on some models the bolt may be too long to completely remove. You don't have to take the bolt out all the way unless it is damaged.

To install the starter

To install a new starter, first make sure the starter and transmission-housing mounting surfaces are clean. This provides the ground circuit for the starter. If you don't have a good ground, the starter will draw off more current than it should and run down the battery. A poor ground can also prevent the starter from cranking. Continuous cranking under these conditions can burn out the starter motor.

1 Install the mounting bolts and torque them to 32 foot pounds.

2 Replace all the wires you removed and tighten the nuts.

3 Reconnect the positive battery cable first, then the negative cable.

It may not be the starter

VOLTMETER   AMMETER   TACHOMETER

10.5 VOLTS   145 AMPS   375 RPM

TO BATTERY   TO BATTERY   TO DISTRIBUTOR   TO GROUND

If any of these test results is not met, it could be an indication that the starter is faulty. But there are other possibilities you should consider.

1 With the remote starter switch or the jumper wire hooked up, if the starter does not start, replace it. However, a no-start condition with the ignition switch but the starter energizing and engaging properly with the remote starter or jumper wire means the starter and solenoid are OK. The problem may be in the ignition switch itself, or in the wiring circuit, or, on Hondamatic-equipped cars, the neutral safety/back-up switch. If the starter does not crank the engine steadily or smoothly, the starter should be considered for replacement, but don't forget to check the engine flywheel as a possible source of the problem.

2 If amperage draw is higher than specifications, the starter is probably faulty, more specifically the armature. But, it is possible for the engine to have too much drag.
3 If the voltage reading is below specifications and the amperage reading is high, there is a good possibility that the starter is faulty—most likely the commutator part of the armature. However, a discharged battery will also yield less than specifications during the cranking test.
4 If engine speed is less than 300 rpm during the cranking test and is coupled with high amperage draw and low voltage reading, it is a good indication of a faulty starter. But, loose connections at the starter or battery positive or negative terminals could be the cause. Also, a tight or binding engine due to lack of lubrication could be the cause.

Warm engine

Disable ignition

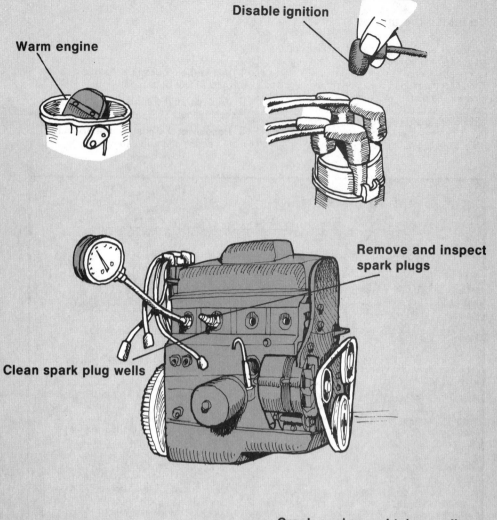

Remove and inspect spark plugs

Clean spark plug wells

Crank engine and take readings

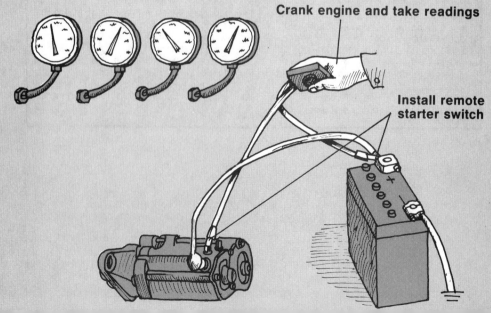

Install remote starter switch

5
Compression Service

PREP: Check the engine oil. If it is very old, dirty, diluted with gasoline or not at the proper level, the compression readings will be affected (p. 43). Check the battery. The starter cranks the engine during a compression test, and a weak battery can't keep the engine cranking fast enough to give accurate readings (p. 10).

1 Warm engine. The test should be performed with the engine at normal operating temperature or at least 63°C (150°F) (p. 40). Also remove the air cleaner (p. 40).

2 Clean spark plug wells. This is a precaution which prevents dirt from entering the cylinders when the spark plugs are removed (p. 40).

3 Remove and inspect spark plugs. Remove the plugs from the cylinder head, marking them with a code to insure correct reinstallation (p. 41).

4 Disable ignition. To prevent the engine from starting during the test, remove the coil wire from the center of the distributor cap and ground it with a jumper wire (p. 41).

5 Install remote starter switch. If you don't have a helper to crank the engine over from inside the car, you'll need a remote starter switch (p. 42).

6 Crank engine and take readings. Crank the engine for four compression strokes to obtain the highest reading. Write down the cylinder number and the reading. Repeat the test for all cylinders (p. 42).

Essential. Basic tools • Spark plug wrench
• Compression gauge • Masking tape •
Jumper wire • Paper and pencil.
Handy. Fender cover • Remote starter switch
• Spark plug cable remover • Ratchet set.

Warm engine

On 1978–79 Accords, 1979 Preludes, and all
1980 Hondas, the choke blade is controlled by
an automatic choke coil and housing. Other
Hondas have a manual choke.

1 Let the engine run until it reaches normal
operating temperature or at least 63°C
(150°F). This is to reduce the friction and
other interactions of a cold engine. Your
Honda is equipped with a temperature gauge
and you should be familiar with the normal
operating range for your car.

2 Remove the air cleaner.

*CAUTION: The compression test is
performed on a warm engine. Many of the
engine parts are hot and some can exceed
the temperature at which water boils,
especially the intake manifold, exhaust
manifold, and even the spark plugs, so take
care not to burn your hands.*

CHOKE
BLADE

**3 The choke blade on later models
should be fully opened.** On Hondas with a
manual choke, the choke knob should be
pushed all the way in and the choke butterfly
valve fully opened.

4 Turn the engine off once it is warm.

Clean spark plug wells

Dirt, sand, and grease that gather around the
base of the spark plugs can fall into the cylinders and cause damage when the plugs are
removed. Professional mechanics use compressed air to blow the dirt away. You can blow
through a medium-length ¼-inch rubber hose

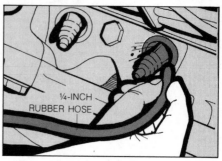

¼-INCH
RUBBER HOSE

to loosen the dirt around the base of the plugs,
then take out all of the plugs. Another way is
to let the engine do it for you.

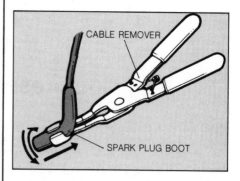

CABLE REMOVER

SPARK PLUG BOOT

1 Remove the spark plug cables by
twisting the boots back and forth with a cable
remover to free them from the plugs and then
pulling on the boot only.

2 Loosen the spark plugs using a ratchet
set: a handle, an extension, a U-joint, and a
spark plug socket. Loosen all the plugs one
turn counterclockwise.
🛑 Keep the socket as straight as possible
because the top of the plug is made of
porcelain and too much angle may cause the
plug to break.

3 Reconnect the cables.

4 Start the engine and let it run for one
minute. Engine compression leaking past the
spark plugs should blow away any dirt in the
plug wells as well as clean the carbon from
the spark plug threads.

5 Now shut off the engine.

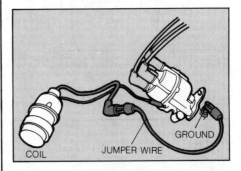

PRO SHOP Honda original-equipment and Honda replacement spark-plug wires are already numbered in yellow, but it can be difficult to see. So you may wish to use masking tape and number each cylinder and similarly code each cable in succession for identification when reconnecting them.

Remove and inspect spark plugs

1 Remove the coded plug wires again.

2 Carefully take out the spark plugs and mark them with the same code as the cables to ensure correct reinstallation.

3 Inspect the plugs for worn or burned electrodes, improper gap, cracked ceramic or electrode insulators, and carbon or oil fouling. See the chapter on Spark Plug Service for a complete, illustrated discussion of how to inspect plugs.

4 Clean the plugs before reinstalling them after making the compression test. Reinstall them into the cylinder head finger-tight and then torque them to 14 foot pounds or about ¼-turn.

Disable ignition

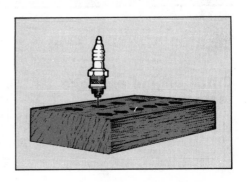

1 Ground the secondary ignition system by removing the high voltage wire from the center of the distributor cap.

2 Attach one end of the jumper wire to the metal terminal of the high voltage wire and the other end to a convenient bolt or nut on the shock tower or engine. This will ground the ignition system and prevent it from operating and being damaged.

PRO SHOP You can make your own plug holder. If the spark plugs are to be reused, they should be stored in a safe place to prevent damage to the porcelain or outer electrode. You can put them in a drilled block of wood, an egg carton or push them into a piece of heavy cardboard.

Install remote starter switch

If you don't have a helper to crank the engine over from inside the car, you'll need to hook up a remote starter switch. Following the instructions which come with the switch, connect one lead to the starter switch terminal of the solenoid. Connect the other lead to the positive terminal on the battery.

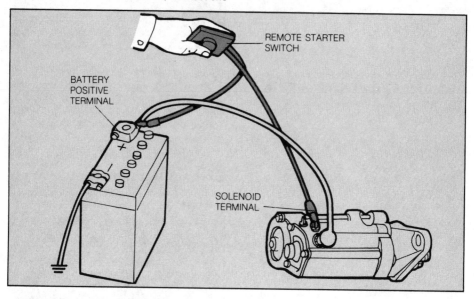

REMOTE STARTER SWITCH

BATTERY POSITIVE TERMINAL

SOLENOID TERMINAL

Compression gauges

Two types of compression gauges are in general use. The more common push-in type works on most cars. To use this type gauge, you need easily accessible spark plug holes which most Hondas have. The exceptions are some CVCC sedans and wagon models from 1975–79 equipped with air conditioning. With the push-in type gauge, you have to hold the rubber grommet end over the spark plug hole, and in most cases this requires a helper.

The other and more expensive type of compression gauge is the screw-in type. This type is more common and much handier for difficult-to-reach spark plug port locations. It usually has a flexible hose and adapter which will thread into Honda spark plug ports. To use either type, follow the manufacturer's instructions.

Crank engine and take readings

To record the readings for comparison later, have a pencil and pad ready. Draw a chart of the engine's cylinder sequence to record the corresponding compression reading.

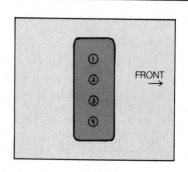

FRONT →

1 Open the carburetor throttle plates.
Your helper can do this by pressing the accelerator pedal to the floor or you can use a brick or cut and wedge a piece of wood on the gas pedal.

2 Crank the engine for four compression strokes (approximately four seconds) with the gauge in place to obtain the highest reading. Record the reading of this cylinder on your chart. Repeat this test procedure for all cylinders and record the readings as you go.

🛑 Do not pump the pedal during the test or gasoline will get into the cylinders and wash the oil off their walls, thereby giving false readings.

PRO SHOP An easy way to count compression strokes if you're using a gauge with a grommet seal is to watch the needle. It will move every time there is a compression stroke. If you're using a screw-in type, the gauge's hose will move each time the engine goes through a compression stroke.

Test conclusions

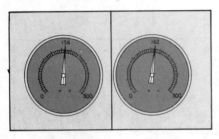

These gauges show ideal compressions of 158 and 162 psi. On all Hondas between 1973 and 1980, except the 1980 Civic with the 1500cc engine, ideal compression is around 160 psi on all four cylinders. The 1980 Civic with the 1500cc engine would have an ideal reading of 180 psi on all four cylinders.

Compare your compression readings with the manufacturer's specifications chart. Maximum variation between the highest and lowest cylinder readings on your Honda must not exceed 28 psi. Put another way, all the readings should be no lower than 75 percent of the highest reading.

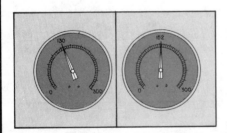

Although these readings are within an acceptable limit, this much difference could be an indication that a problem is developing. Repeat the compression test to make sure you did not make a mistake. If the readings are the same, recheck the compression after a couple thousand miles, and if the readings still vary as much, you may want to ask the advice of a professional mechanic.

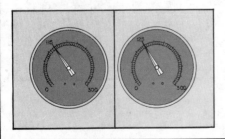

Compression readings of 125 and 115 psi are lower than Honda minimum specifications, but if the other two cylinders' readings are between these, then the readings are uniform and no cylinder has a compression lower than 110 psi. If the engine is not using an excessive quantity of oil, it is considered tuneable, but performance and economy will not be at their maximum.

| MODEL | YEAR | COMPRESSION SPECIFICATIONS CHART | | |
		MEAN COMPRESSION	MINIMUM COMPRESSION	MAXIMUM VARIATION
Civic 1200	1973–1977	156	128	28
CVCC	1975–1979	164	136	28
Civic 1200	1978–1979	164	136	28
Accords	1976–1979	164	136	28
Accords & Preludes	1979–1980	156	128	28
Civic 1500	1980	185	156	28
Civic 1300	1980	156	128	28

What the readings mean

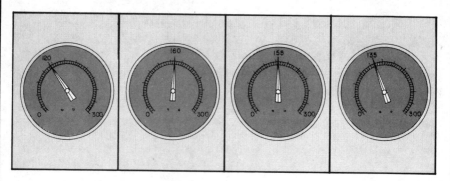

Good compression readings mean that the piston rings and valves are mechanically capable of compressing the fuel-and-air mixture.

If the readings are low or uneven in any of the cylinders, add several squirts of engine oil through each of the spark plug openings. Do not inject more than about

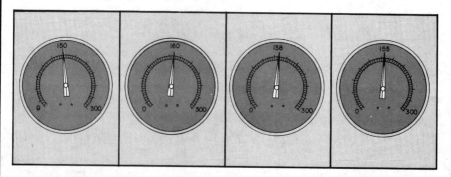

one tablespoon into each cylinder. Crank the engine over three or four times. Now recheck and record the compression.

If it improves by 20 psi or more, the piston rings are probably worn. If the compression

What the readings mean (continued)

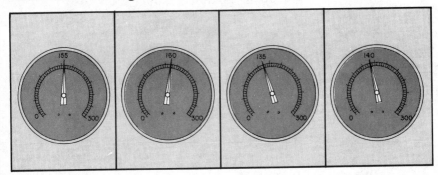

does not improve, the valves are probably sticking, seating poorly, or are burned.

If two cylinders next to each other show readings of more than 20 pounds lower than the others and injecting oil doesn't change the readings, then the head gasket could be bad.

Suspect a blown head gasket on a Honda

if the engine is overheating, the coolant level continues dropping, the oil becomes milky or on the first start-up in the morning a large amount of white smoke billows out the tailpipe (not to be confused with normal condensation smoke). However, faulty head gaskets are rare on newer model cars.

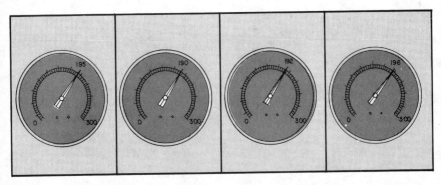

If all the cylinders read exceptionally high, then it's likely there are excessive carbon deposits inside the combustion chamber. To confirm this, warm up the engine and ground the distributor wire from the ignition coil. If the engine attempts to start, then there are probably carbon deposits.

If your engine shows low compression (less than 110 psi), uneven compression or abnormally high compression readings, in-

ternal engine repair work is probably necessary and there is no point in proceeding with a tune-up. You should see a professional mechanic.

When you have finished testing the compression, shut off the ignition switch and make sure the carburetor plates are closed. Remove all gauges and reinstall the spark plugs and wires. Start the engine and make sure it runs OK as a check that everything is hooked up properly.

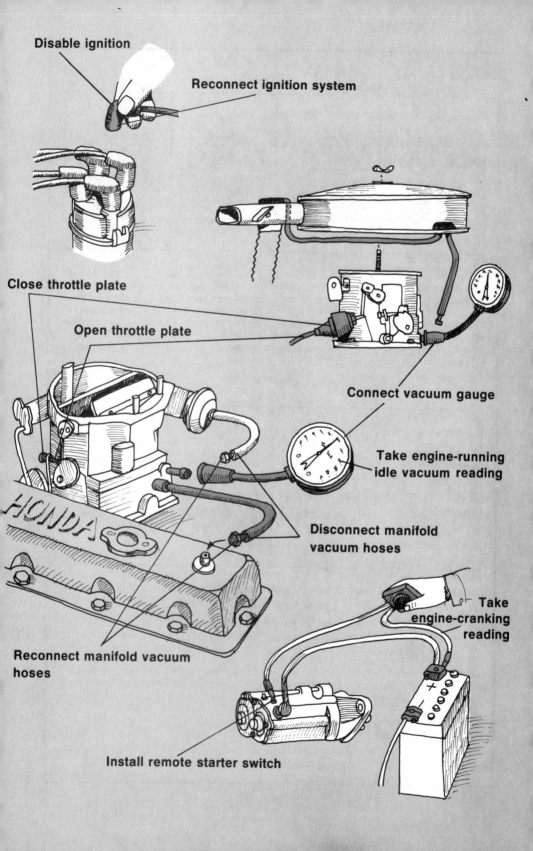

Disable ignition

Reconnect ignition system

Close throttle plate

Open throttle plate

Connect vacuum gauge

Take engine-running idle vacuum reading

HONDA

Disconnect manifold vacuum hoses

Reconnect manifold vacuum hoses

Take engine-cranking reading

Install remote starter switch

6
Vacuum Service

PREP: Check the battery. It must have sufficient charge to crank the engine (p. 10). Warm the engine. It should be at normal operating temperature or at least 60°C (150°F). Check the oil. The engine oil should be at the proper level and in good condition to properly seal the rings (p. 48).

1 Connect vacuum gauge. The gauge is attached to a source of manifold vacuum. The only source of manifold vacuum on the CVCC engine is the insulator block. On the Civic 1200, manifold vacuum reading is obtained from the insulator block or the manifold itself (p. 48).

2 Take engine-running idle vacuum reading. Record the idle reading for later comparison with the cranking vacuum reading. See "What the readings mean" (p. 49). Shut off the engine.

3 Disable ignition. This is done so the vacuum reading may be taken with the engine cranking, not running (p. 51).

4 Install remote starter switch. If you don't have a helper to crank the engine, you'll need a remote starter switch (p. 51).

5 Close throttle plate. To close the carburetor throttle plate, back off the throttle stop screw (idle speed adjustment screw) (p. 51).

6 Disconnect manifold vacuum hoses. For an accurate engine-cranking reading, you must remove, code, and plug manifold vacuum sources (p. 53).

7 Take engine-cranking reading. Observe the vacuum gauge while cranking the engine. A normal reading will be equal to or greater than the engine-running vacuum reading. If your readings are not within specs, see "What the readings mean" (p. 54).

8 Reconnect manifold vacuum hoses. Carefully reconnect vacuum hoses and retest running vacuum to check for proper operation (p. 55).

9 Open throttle plate. The engine must idle at the normal speed. Check with a tachometer if necessary (p. 55).

10 Reconnect ignition system. Remove the ground from the coil wire (p. 55).

Essential. Basic tools • Jumper wire • Manifold vacuum gauge • Masking tape • Paper and pencil.
Handy. Fender cover • Remote starter switch • Tachometer.

Connect vacuum gauge

Attach the vacuum gauge hose to a source of intake manifold vacuum following the gauge manufacturer's instructions. Manifold vacuum sources are always at a point below the throttle plates.

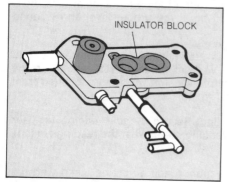

On 1975–79 Hondas with the CVCC engine, the best location for manifold vacuum source is one of the smaller connections off the four-way joint (or five-way joint on 1980 Civics, Accords, and Preludes).

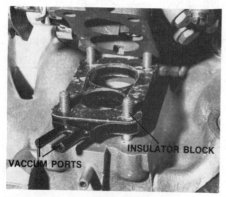

On the Civic 1200, there are two main sources of manifold vacuum. From 1973–77, the source is on this type of insulator block.

In 1978 and 1979, the Civic 1200 insulator block took on a different shape. And on the Hondamatic-equipped models in 1978 and 1979, one of the ports has no vacuum hose nor vacuum at that port. Note: The insulator blocks used on Hondas, whether the Civic or CVCC, are all made of a darkened bakalite material and are located between the intake manifold and the carburetor.

The main source of vacuum on the 1973 and 1974 Civic 1200 models is the manifold itself. Unlike the CVCC models that have no ports in the intake manifold, these models have two manifold vacuum ports.

On the 1975–79 Civic manifolds, there are several vacuum sources. It is best to use one of the smaller ports because they are more accessible.

Take engine-running idle vacuum reading

1 With the vacuum gauge hooked up and all standard safety precautions taken, start the engine. If it is not warm, let it idle until it reaches normal operating temperature.

2 Observe and record your idle vacuum for evaluation and later comparison with the engine-cranking reading. The vacuum reading should be high and steady (between 17 and 21 inches of vacuum). This reading at idle indicates that the engine is mechanically sound—it has good rings and a properly sealed combusion chamber and intake manifold.

What is vacuum in the engine?

Vacuum is negative pressure created in the engine by the pistons. The pistons are initially forced up and down by their indirect connection to the flywheel, which is turned by the starter. As a piston goes down, it draws a vacuum. In the engine, the intake valve opens and allows this vacuum to be drawn through the intake manifold and the carburetor. This draws a calibrated amount of the fuel-and-air mixture into the engine. The running of the engine continues the constant draw of vacuum by the pistons.

A good engine vacuum reading at sea level ranges from 16 to 22 inches. This decreases about one inch for every 1,000 feet of altitude above sea level. For example, if you live in a coastal or sea level area, a good idle manifold vacuum reading on your Honda would be 17 to 21 inches. An idle manifold vacuum reading of 12 to 17 inches would be acceptable if you live at an elevation of 5,000 feet above sea level.

What the readings mean

Engine-running vacuum test

A radically fluctuating needle of eight to ten inches as speed is increased or at a running rpm indicates cylinder head gasket leakage. With your engine running, the vacuum reading will drop sharply each time the leak occurs, from a steady reading to a reading of eight to ten inches or less. When the leak is between two adjacent cylinders, the drop will be much greater. You can locate the leak by taking a compression gauge test. An intake manifold

leak or manifold gasket leak at just one of the intake ports or a leaking or burned valve could also cause this type of reading. A severe engine miss will also cause the vacuum needle to fluctuate but normally not as radically.

A high steady reading between 17 and 21 inches is normal and indicates that the engine is mechanically sound.

What the readings mean (continued)

A fluctuation of an inch or two inter-mittently indicates a sticking valve. You can make this test at a slow idle speed. Each time the valve closes but doesn't seat properly, the vacuum reading will drop an inch or more. This happens as each leaky valve fails to seal. The valve or valves causing this can be located by performing the compression gauge test. An ignition miss may also cause your vacuum gauge to fluctuate intermittently.

If the vacuum gauge vibrates an inch or so above or below normal, you probably have ignition problems. If, with the engine idling, you get continued needle vibration about an inch to an inch and a half above or below an acceptable reading, it may be caused by defective spark plugs, improper spark plug gap, faulty point adjustment, spark plug wire leaks, a bad distributor cap or a weak ignition coil. Further testing with electrical equipment is required in this case.

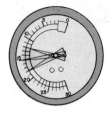

A constant fluctuation between three and eight inches with the engine idling and the gauge below normal indicates an intake system leak. This reading may mean a leak through the intake manifold gaskets, the carburetor base gaskets or any vacuum-operated accessories such as vacuum power assisted brakes.

A gauge reading that gradually drops, especially if the engine is held at a stable 3000 rpm, is an indication of excessive back pressure in the exhaust system.

A vacuum reading that is higher than normal and also steady is an indication of over-advanced ignition timing. This condition can best be checked with a timing light.

A needle that drifts from normal to several inches below normal and back again usually suggests an improper idle mixture adjustment. An idle drop adjustment of the fuel-and-air mixture and adjustment of idle speed to specifications should correct this condition. This type of reading can also be caused by a minor vacuum leak.

Disable ignition

Cranking vacuum is a valuable diagnostic test that can be used to determine the condition of the engine and the intake system. The vacuum reading is taken with the engine cranking, not running, so it is necessary to disable the ignition.

Remove the coil high-tension wire from the distributor cap and connect a jumper from this wire to a suitable ground (see the chapter on Starting System Service).

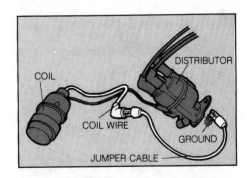

Install remote starter switch

If you don't have a helper to crank the engine, you'll need a remote starter switch. The remote starter switch hook-up is discussed at length in the chapter on Starter System Service. It simply involves following the manufacturer's instructions: Connect one lead to the battery positive terminal and the other lead to the solenoid switch terminal.
CAUTION: remember that with this hook-up the car can lunge forward or backward. So if it is in gear, follow all safety precautions.

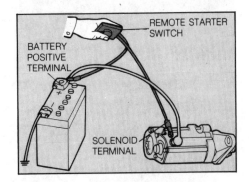

Close throttle plate

On all Hondas, the throttle plate is closed by simply backing off the throttle stop screw (idle-speed adjustment screw) in a counterclockwise direction until the throttle is completely closed. Count the number of turns necessary to do this so you can correctly reset the idle later. If the throttle plate is held open during cranking, the vacuum reading will be inaccurate. So on Hondas with manual chokes, make sure the choke is pushed in. On models with automatic chokes, be sure the choke is warm and not engaged.

On 1973–76 Civic 1200's, the throttle stop screw is located on the left (driver) side of the carburetor and is fairly easy to see.

On 1977–79 Civic 1200's, the screw is more difficult to locate and turn, especially with the air-cleaner case installed. On these models, the screw is on the right (passenger) side of the carburetor behind the choke linkage.

On 1975–77 CVCC sedans and wagons and 1976 and 1977 Accords, the screw can be seen only by removing the air-cleaner case. On these models, the screw is located at the firewall side of the carburetor to the right (passenger) side of center.

On 1978 and 1979 sedans and wagons, 1978 and 1979 Accords, 1979 Preludes, and all 1980 Hondas, the throttle stop screw is located in the same place as on the earlier CVCC models. That is, on the back of the carburetor to the right of center. But the screw on these models has a black knob. You must remove the air-cleaner case to locate the screw, especially on 1980 models which have additional hoses behind the carburetor.

Disconnect manifold vacuum hoses

If you have looked under the hood of your Honda, you have already noticed a large number of hoses. Many of these are vacuum hoses. Some control emission devices and others operate vacuum-controlled accessories such as power-assisted brakes. Any of these vacuum controls could be a source of vacuum bleed-off. When you perform the engine-cranking test, this bleed-off will cause an inaccurate engine-cranking reading. So to ensure an accurate reading, you must remove and plug all manifold vacuum sources except for the vacuum gauge, which can be put on one of the ports of the insulator block.

One method of removing and plugging vacuum sources is to make some vacuum plugs. Take short lengths (two inches) of ⅛-inch inside-diameter hose. Put a screw into one end of the plug and install it on the vacuum port. Some of the larger ports will require two-inch lengths of ⁵/₁₆-inch inside-diameter hose. To make sure you reinstall the hoses in their proper position, remove and code the hoses and ports with pieces of masking tape.

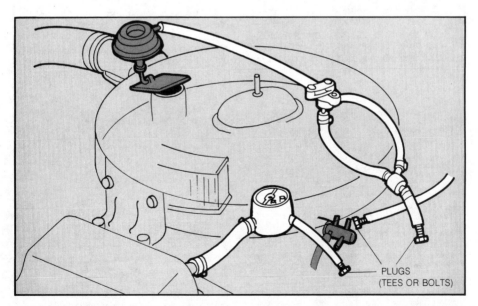

PLUGS
(TEES OR BOLTS)

Another method is to go to the vacuum unit itself, disconnect and code the vacuum hose, and install a screw or a plug to stop vacuum bleed-off. This method is sometimes more difficult, especially on the Civic 1200 where some of the vacuum units are hard to reach.

Take engine-cranking reading

Observe the vacuum gauge needle while cranking the engine. Note and record the gauge reading for comparison with the engine-running reading taken already. The cranking test will monitor the level of the vacuum in the intake manifold and its consistency. The engine-cranking reading should be equal to or greater than the engine-running reading. Now compare your readings with "What the readings mean." Note: Vacuum gauge readings may pulsate very slightly, especially if all vacuum ports are not plugged.

What the readings mean

Engine-cranking vacuum test

A very low engine-cranking vacuum indicates a vacuum leak somewhere between the piston and the carburetor throttle plate. The most common place for a vacuum leak of this magnitude is in the gasket area between the intake manifold and the head.

An uneven, pulsating gauge needle movement indicates faulty valves, rings, pistons, head gasket or uneven cranking speed. Uneven cranking speed can mean uneven compression. Note: If you find your engine has low or uneven cranking vacuum, perform a compression test if you haven't already done so. You cannot successfully tune your engine until compression or vacuum leaks are corrected.

Low, even gauge needle movement indicates low compression, incorrect valve timing, throttle plate not closed tightly or vacuum leaks at intake valve guides. This can also be an indication of slow cranking speed which could be related to the starter and/or battery.

PRO SHOP An intake manifold vacuum leak will cause an engine to run and idle rough no matter how finely the carburetor is adjusted. If you suspect an intake manifold vacuum leak, here's how to detect it: With the engine running, place some light engine oil around the surfaces where the intake manifold meets the cylinder head. If the engine idle noticeably smoothes out, there is indeed a vacuum leak at one of the intake manifold contact surfaces.

Reconnect manifold vacuum hoses

1 Make sure the hoses are on all the way.

2 Reinstall the spring clamps if they were used on your model.

3 Check the hoses to make sure they are not split, cracked or deteriorated. If so, you should replace them. After all the hoses have been hooked up, retest the running vacuum to make sure the engine is operating OK.

Open throttle plate

For the engine to idle at the proper speed, the throttle plate must be open. Turn the idle-speed screw clockwise the same number of turns you backed it off when you closed the plate. To ensure proper idle, especially if any repairs were made, it is best to hook up a tachometer and compare the idle speed with the manufacturer's specifications, then reset if necessary.

Reconnect ignition system

1 Remove the jumper wire from the coil high-tension wire and its ground.

2 Reinstall the coil wire into the center of the distributor cap.

ECONOTIP Of all the things car engineers can do to improve gas mileage, the biggest improvement comes from weight reduction. When you buy a car, remember that no matter how good and careful a driver you are, a heavier car will not get as good mileage as a lighter car, if everything else is equal. There are some small car engines of older design which are not very efficient. In that case, a later model heavier car might get better mileage. But if you want to be a champion in the miles-per-gallon race, the lightest car with a modern engine will be a winner.

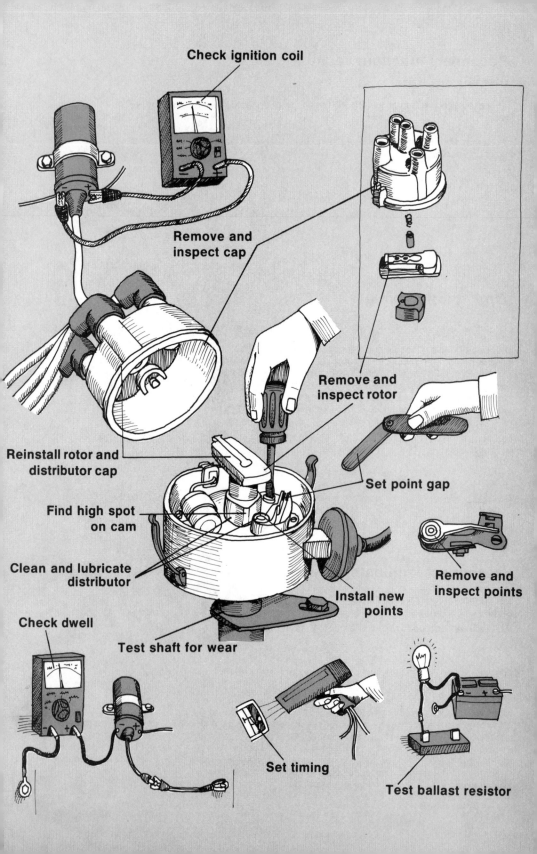

Check ignition coil

Remove and inspect cap

Remove and inspect rotor

Reinstall rotor and distributor cap

Set point gap

Find high spot on cam

Clean and lubricate distributor

Remove and inspect points

Install new points

Check dwell

Test shaft for wear

Set timing

Test ballast resistor

7

Distributor Service

1 **Remove and inspect cap.** Look for cracks and burned or corroded terminals. Remove the cables and inspect the towers (p. 58).

2 **Remove and inspect rotor.** Look for cracks, corrosion, and burns (p. 59). If your Honda is equipped with electronic ignition (1979 Accords and Preludes and all 1980 Hondas), proceed to the section on electronic ignitions (p. 72).

3 **Remove and inspect points.** If they are pitted, burned or the rubbing block is worn, replace them. Replace the condenser when replacing the points (p. 59).

4 **Clean and lubricate distributor.** Wipe the breaker plate and cam clean. Apply a light coating of cam lube to the cam (p. 61).

5 **Install new points.** Position the points on the breaker plate and tighten the holding screws finger-tight (p. 62).

6 **Find high spot on cam.** Install a remote starter switch (p. 28), have a helper crank the engine or turn the engine over by hand (p. 62).

7 **Set point gap.** Adjust the gap with a feeler gauge and tighten the holding screws (p. 63).

8 **Test shaft for wear.** Push the distributor shaft from side to side. If the point gap increases or decreases, the distributor is worn (p. 64).

9 **Reinstall rotor and distributor cap.** Make sure the rotor is properly seated. Position the cap correctly and fasten it to the distributor (p. 64).

10 **Check dwell.** Measure the point gap with a dwell meter (p. 65). On cars with electronic ignition dwell is not adjustable.

11 **Set timing.** Connect a timing light to the number 1 spark plug wire and set the timing. Check the vacuum advance (p. 66).

12 **Test ballast resistor.** This can easily be done with a test light, but a more accurate test is done with an ohmmeter (p. 70).

13 **Check ignition coil.** Clean the coil tower when servicing the distributor. Test the coil with an ohmmeter and replace it if it is damaged (p. 71).

Essential. Basic tools • Feeler gauge • Ignition wrench (8-mm) • Cam lube • Timing light • Towels or clean rags • Droplight or flashlight • Tachometer.
Handy. Remote starter switch • Dwell meter • Magnetic screwdriver • Ohmmeter • Test light • Hand vacuum pump.

Remove and inspect cap

SPRING CLIP

1 Remove the distributor cap. It is attached to the distributor base with spring clips. To remove these clips, insert a screwdriver blade between the cap and the spring clip and twist.

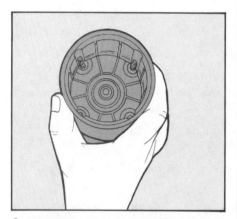

2 Clean the cap to remove grease and dirt from the outside. Use a droplight or flashlight when inspecting the cap. Check the outside and inside for cracks, carbon tracks, corrosion, and burned terminals. If you find any of these, replace the cap. Now look at the center electrode to make sure it hasn't worn away.

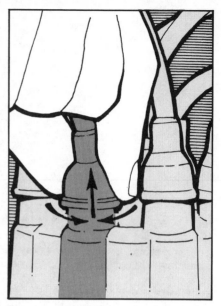

3 Remove the spark plug cables one at a time from the top of the cap and clean and inspect them. Never pull on the wires when removing them. Twist the boot one-half a turn in each direction to free it from the tower and the wire ends.

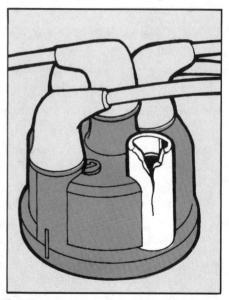

4 Check the condition of the distributor cap tower for cracks and corrosion and replace it if necessary. A worn cap can cause hard starting, engine misfiring, and can even prevent starting altogether.

Remove and inspect rotor

1 To remove the rotor, simply lift straight up on it. Rotors are press-fitted to the center shaft of the distributor.

2 Inspect the rotor for cracks, chips, corrosion, burns or weak spring tension. Be sure to turn it over and inspect the underside with a flashlight for electrical tracking (indicated by black lines on the surface). You should replace a rotor with any of the above conditions. Always replace both the rotor and the cap.

To replace rotor

To replace the rotor and cap, you must transfer the spark plug wires from the old cap to the new one.

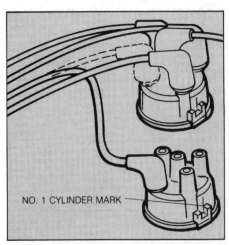

1 Align the number 1 cylinder mark on new and replacement Honda caps. Use that mark as a starting point.

2 Then remove one wire at a time from the old cap and install it in the same tower of the new cap. If your car is equipped with electronic ignition, proceed to the discussion in this chapter on electronic ignitions.

Remove and inspect points

1 To remove the points, make sure the ignition key is in the off position.

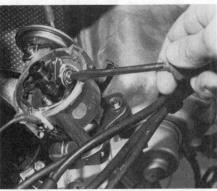

2 Now loosen the primary wire screw and remove the wire. Note: It is usually not necessary to remove this screw or the screw holding the contact set (points) in place. But in some cases you may have to remove the contact set before the primary wire screw can be loosened.

3 To remove the contact set itself, just loosen the two hold-down screws and tilt the point set up on the outside edge and slide it out from under the screws. You shouldn't have to remove the screws.

4 Inspect the points for wear. If they are pitted, worn, loose or blue in color, the rubbing block worn or the pivot point damaged, you should replace them. If the points are light gray and have a smooth surface, they can be reused. Any time you replace the contact set, you should replace the condenser.

PRO SHOP Distributors in Civic 1200's from 1973–79 go into the front of the engine sideways between the engine and the firewall. A magnetic screwdriver is very handy here. In fact, many professional mechanics remove the distributor from these models in order to more easily remove the contact set and the condenser.

ECONOTIP A properly tuned car is a must for good gas mileage as is a properly attuned driver. He's conscious of the kind of driving habits that make refueling stops as brief as a race driver's. For good gas mileage, keep the following tips in mind:
• Slow down. While a race driver wins with a lead foot, you don't. Cars are generally more efficient at 55 miles per hour or less.
• Drive smoothly. Try to avoid pumping the throttle and varying your speed. Smooth, even driving is more efficient.
• Avoid tire-squealing starts. You'll be the first away from the traffic light and the first into the gas station.
• Don't ride the brake. Use the brake as little as you safely can. Coasting when possible saves gas.
• Empty the trunk. There's no sense in carrying around excess baggage. It just adds weight.
• Avoid idling. Idling engines are inefficient. If you're going to idle more than a few seconds, shut the engine off.
• Plan ahead. Arrange your trips to get as much done as possible. One trip is more efficient than two.

Breaker-point ignition service tips

Servicing the distributor is easy if you follow these tips:
• Be careful when removing the distributor cap. It's made of plastic and if you pry too hard with your screwdriver, it will break.
• Always check the underside of the rotor for electrical tracking (carbon tracking).
• When replacing a cap or rotor, be sure the new parts are exactly the same size and shape as the old ones. Make sure the rotor is aligned properly and is all the way down on the distributor shaft. The cap must fit the distributor snugly and evenly. Be careful not to damage the rotor when installing the cap over it and always replace the cap and rotor at the same time.

• Do not touch the point contact surfaces with your fingers and avoid getting dirt or oil on them.
• Don't drop the point attaching screws into the distributor.
• Use only cam lube on the distributor cam and don't overlube. If lube gets on the contact points, their life will be shortened.
• Use a clean feeler gauge to set the points.
• Always replace the condenser when replacing the points.
• Keep your hands and the timing light clear of the engine fan when setting the timing.

Clean and lubricate distributor

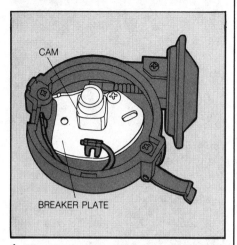

CAM

BREAKER PLATE

1 Wipe the breaker plate and cam clean of dirt and old cam lube.

2 Check the cam lobes for roughness or pitting. If the cam is rough, the points will not stay in adjustment. You should replace the distributor if the cam is damaged.

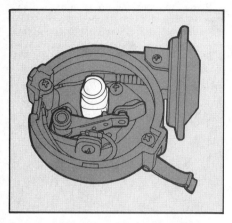

3 Apply a light coating of lube to the cam. Spread not more than two match heads worth equally around it, then wipe off any excess. Note: In the center of the Honda distributor shaft under the plastic cap, there is a small screw and washer, under which you should apply a small amount of multi-purpose grease. This helps lubricate the advance weights' pivot points.

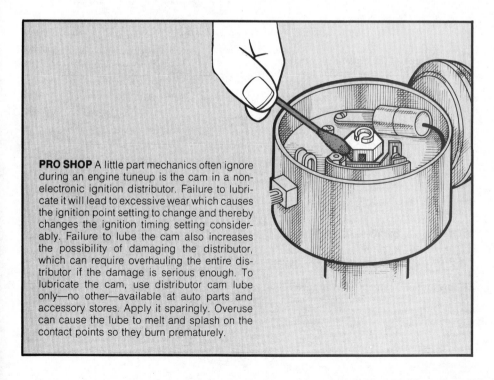

PRO SHOP A little part mechanics often ignore during an engine tuneup is the cam in a non-electronic ignition distributor. Failure to lubricate it will lead to excessive wear which causes the ignition point setting to change and thereby changes the ignition timing setting considerably. Failure to lube the cam also increases the possibility of damaging the distributor, which can require overhauling the entire distributor if the damage is serious enough. To lubricate the cam, use distributor cam lube only—no other—available at auto parts and accessory stores. Apply it sparingly. Overuse can cause the lube to melt and splash on the contact points so they burn prematurely.

Install new points

1 Place the points on the distributor breaker plate and tighten the hold-down screws finger-tight. Be sure the locating pin (part of the pivot point) lines up with the hole in the breaker plate and that the point set sits flat. Be careful that no grease or dirt gets on the point surfaces.

STOP Before installing a new ignition point set, check to see if the points are in proper alignment with each other. If not, carefully bend the point brace with needlenose pliers.

LOCATING PIN

2 Now install a new condenser. Note: Almost all Hondas from 1973–79 with non-electronic ignitions have an externally mounted condenser. Exceptions are the CVCC-equipped 1975 and 1976 models with Hondamatic transmissions and the CVCC-equipped 1976 and 1977 Hondas in California and high-altitude sales areas. On these models, the condenser is inside the distributor on the breaker plate.

EXTERNAL CONDENSER

For both types of condenser mountings, the primary wire from the contact set must connect to the terminal in the side of the distributor which hooks up to the distributor (negative) side of the coil. The wire terminal and connector going through the side of the distributor must be clean, tight, and properly connected. Be sure not to drop the square nut on the inside into the distributor.

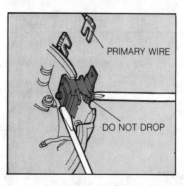

PRIMARY WIRE

DO NOT DROP

Find high spot on cam

1 Position the distributor cam so the high spot is against the rubbing block.

2 Now install a remote starter switch (see the chapter on Starting System Service) or have a helper crank the engine, with short bursts, until the high spot of the cam is in position. The high spot is where the points are open widest.

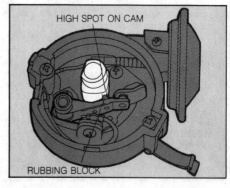

HIGH SPOT ON CAM

RUBBING BLOCK

Reposition cam

On the Honda, the easiest way to reposition the cam may be to turn the engine over by hand. You can do this by turning the front crank pulley nut counterclockwise until the high spot on the cam rests against the rubbing block. You will need the proper size socket and an extension with a rachet.

To find the front crank pulley nut, turn the front wheels to the left and look into the wheel well behind the driver's side tire. At the lower center there is a round rubber plug that can be removed, giving you access to the front crank pulley nut.

Set point gap

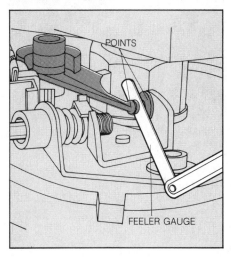

POINTS

FEELER GAUGE

Measure the gap between the two point faces with a clean feeler gauge. Adjust the gap until it meets specifications, which on all non-electronic ignition Hondas is about 0.48 mm (.020 of an inch). The point gap is changed by moving the points toward or away from the distributor cam.

1 With the hold-down screws finger-tight, turn the center adjusting screw until the points are properly set.

2 After tightening the hold-down screws, recheck the gap to make sure it hasn't moved.

Keep the feeler clean

Anyone doing his own engine tuneup knows that the distributor breaker points should be kept as clean as possible. Otherwise, they burn prematurely. However, sometimes do-it-yourselfers make a slip and pick up a feeler gauge which looks as if it had been used as an oil dipstick. Oil or grease is then deposited on the points, and before you know it, you are wondering why the points have gone pf-f-ft. Before slipping the feeler gauge between the points, wipe it off. If the blades won't come clean with a simple wipe, wash them in cleaning solvent and then rinse in water. Be sure the gauge is dry before using it.

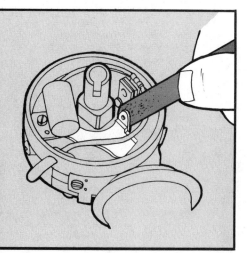

Test shaft for wear

1 With the rubbing block still in contact with the high spot on the cam, push the distributor shaft in the direction of the block.

2 Look for side-to-side play in the distributor shaft. If the shaft moves and the point gap increases by more than .010 inches, the distributor is worn and will probably need replacing. But before you do, have it checked by a professional mechanic.

Reinstall rotor and distributor cap

1 Align the press-on-type rotor with the flat side of the distributor shaft. The rotor has a second flat side, but it is not used for alignment. Make sure the rotor is properly seated.

2 Make sure the tab on the distributor lines up with the corresponding locating slot in the cap and that the cap is positioned correctly.

3 Fasten the spring clips.

About dwell meters

Adjusting ignition points by using a tach-dwell meter is a more accurate method of adjusting the points than using a feeler gauge. A dwell meter electronically determines how long the points remain closed and converts that information into the numbers or degrees of distributor rotation. The point gap directly affects dwell. Dwell is the number of degrees the cam rotates between the time that the points close until they reopen again. A dwell reading greater than specifications means the point gap is too narrow and the space between the points needs to be opened up. A dwell reading below specs means the point gap is too wide and the space between the points needs to be closed. Correct dwell is important for ignition system performance. If the dwell is off, the coil won't operate as efficiently as it should.

A dwell meter has two wires. One is hooked to the coil at the primary terminal marked (neg), (−), or (Dist.). The other wire is hooked to a ground such as the negative (−) terminal of the battery or a metal part of the engine such as the manifold bolt head. Once the wires are hooked up, select the proper scale by turning the switch to 4 for the four cylinders on your Honda. Start the car and observe the needle. A good dwell reading is within engine specs with the needle steady.

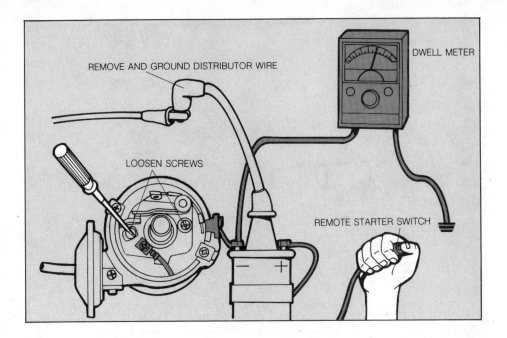

REMOVE AND GROUND DISTRIBUTOR WIRE

DWELL METER

LOOSEN SCREWS

REMOTE STARTER SWITCH

Check dwell

1 Attach a dwell meter according to the manufacturer's instructions. Most dwell meters connect the positive lead of the meter to the negative terminal of the ignition coil on the distributor side. The negative lead goes to the negative post of the battery for a good engine ground.

2 Connect a remote starter switch (as described in the Starting System Service chapter).

3 Remove and ground the distributor wire from the center tower of the distributor cap. *CAUTION: Before you turn the ignition switch on, be sure to follow all safety precautions. Make sure the car is in Park or Neutral and the parking brake is set.*

4 Loosen the hold-down screws just enough to allow for adjustment.

5 Crank the engine with the remote starter switch or have a helper turn the ignition switch to the start position.

6 While the engine is cranking, observe the dwell meter reading and adjust the ignition points and dwell to 52° (between 49° and 55° is acceptable) on all non-electronic ignition system Hondas. This can be done with a screwdriver by turning the adjusting

screw. To reduce the dwell, increase the point gap. To increase the dwell, reduce the gap. This operation should be done as quickly as possible to avoid overheating the starter motor or draining the battery voltage.

7 Release the remote control switch, tighten the ignition point set hold-down screws, and recheck the dwell setting by cranking the engine once again. Reset if necessary. You must reset ignition timing after installing points or setting dwell.

PRO SHOP At this point, replace the air cleaner and start the engine. If you have correctly followed the above procedures for distributor cap and rotor replacement, cam lubrication, points installation, and dwell setting, the engine should start and run reasonably well. If it does not, the difficulty may be one of the following:
• An improperly installed rotor or distributor cap.
• One or more incorrectly attached spark plug wires.
• Spark plug wires switched into the wrong distributor cap tower.
• The primary wire not hooked up properly at the contact set or the distributor terminal.
• The condenser not properly connected.
• Improper point-gap setting (not on the high spot of the cam when set).

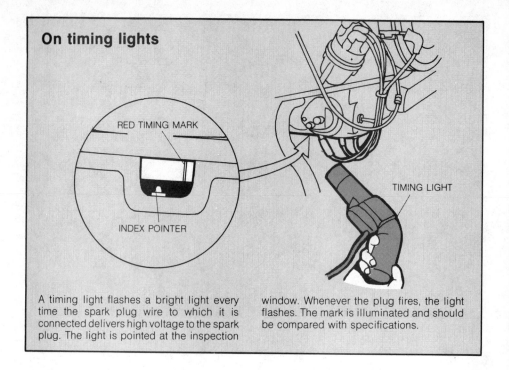

On timing lights

RED TIMING MARK

TIMING LIGHT

INDEX POINTER

A timing light flashes a bright light every time the spark plug wire to which it is connected delivers high voltage to the spark plug. The light is pointed at the inspection window. Whenever the plug fires, the light flashes. The mark is illuminated and should be compared with specifications.

Set timing

Ignition timing is one of the most important adjustments you can make on an engine to improve performance and gas mileage. Timing is adjusted so the spark occurs a specified number of degrees before top dead center (BTDC) or after top dead center (ATDC). Top dead center is the highest point of piston travel in the cylinder. Both mechanical (centrifugal) and vacuum spark advances are based on the specified timing adjustments. If the ignition timing position is off, all the subsequent timing adjustments that are made automatically by the distributor will also be off. After timing is correctly set, shut the engine off.

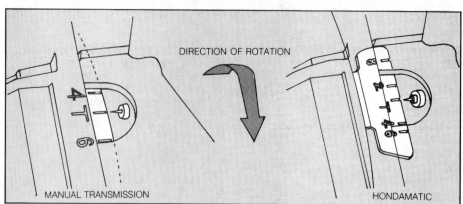

DIRECTION OF ROTATION

MANUAL TRANSMISSION

HONDAMATIC

1 First locate the timing mark. On all CVCC-equipped Hondas from 1975–80, the timing mark is on the flywheel. It may be observed through a hole in the block where the transmission housing meets the block under the number 4 spark plug. You may find a rubber plug in the hole. If so, remove it.

TIMING
MARK

INDICATOR

2 On the Civic 1200 from 1973–79, the timing mark is two lines on the front crank pulley and the indicator is a protrusion from the front timing belt cover. On these models, it may be necessary to clean the pulley marks. Remember the engine rotates in a counterclockwise direction, so, as the marks are up, the red line is the timing mark and the white line is TDC.

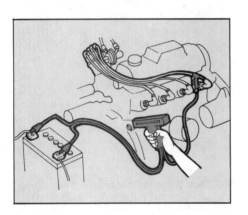

3 Connect your timing light to the engine following the manufacturer's instructions. A typical timing light has three leads. One is connected to the number 1 spark plug wire, one to the positive (+) terminal of the battery, and one to a ground or to the negative (−) terminal on the battery.

4 Compare the timing specs with the EPA (Environmental Protection Agency) sticker. On your Honda, the EPA sticker is located on the underside of the hood. The sticker gives you the basic timing specs for that particular model. It also gives the exact procedure for setting the timing. The proper idle speed is also specified. Follow the procedures on the sticker.

STOP The timing on a Honda is set with the engine at normal operating temperature, at specified idle rpm and with all vacuum hoses connected. All pre-1980 models require that the headlights be on high beam.

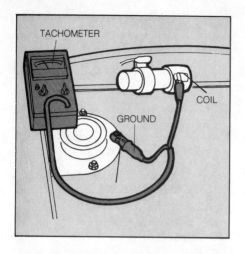

5 Next connect your tachometer to the coil in the engine compartment, following the manufacturer's instructions. A typical tachometer has two leads. One is connected to the distributor side of the coil, the other to a ground such as the negative battery terminal or a body bolt.

6 Check the tachometer for correct engine rpm and aim the timing light at the timing marks. Compare your reading with the specifications.

7 If the timing is not within specs, loosen the distributor hold-down bolt and turn the distributor until the correct timing is indicated. Retighten the hold-down bolt and check the timing to make sure it hasn't moved.

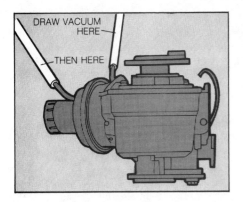

DRAW VACUUM HERE
THEN HERE

8 After the timing is properly set and the distributor is bolted down, if you have a hand-vacuum pump, apply vacuum to the diaphragm. Watch the timing mark with the timing light while applying vacuum to the diaphragm. The mark should move (almost out of sight on the CVCC). On distributors with a dual-vacuum diaphragm, apply vacuum to the inner diaphragm and watch the timing marks move. Apply vacuum to the outer diaphragm. Now the marks should move in the opposite direction. On single-diaphragm distributors, make sure the timing mark moves when vacuum is applied.

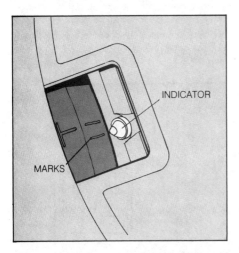

INDICATOR

MARKS

9 After checking the vacuum diaphragms, briefly accelerate the engine while still pointing the timing light at the timing marks. This is now checking the mechanical (centrifugal) advance. The marks will advance beyond the initial setting, probably off the scale again. If either the vacuum diaphragm or the mechanical advance does not move the timing marks, then there is a defect in the system and it should be further tested by a professional mechanic.

Freeing frozen distributors

OIL FILTER WRENCH

One of these days, you're going to unbolt the distributor and try to turn the housing to set the ignition timing, only to find that the housing won't budge—it's frozen. Whatever you do, don't try to loosen it with a hammer. This could damage the distributor. Instead, wrap an oil filter wrench around the housing. This should free it. If it doesn't, squirt some penetrating oil or graphite around the base of the distributor. This should loosen it without causing damage.

Test ballast resistor

Most of the Hondas have a device called a ballast resistor which limits the amount of

BALLAST RESISTOR

current that goes to the ignition system, thus increasing distributor point life. The 1973 Honda and those Hondas with electronic ignition (1979 Accords and Preludes and all 1980 Hondas) have no ballast resistor.

A car with a faulty ballast resistor will usually "start" with the key in the start position, but when the key is released to the "on" position, the engine will stall. On 1974–79 Civic 1200's and on 1975–79 CVCC sedan and wagon models, the ballast resistor and the ignition coil share the same mounting between the shock tower and the firewall. On the 1976–78 Accord models, the ballast resistor is installed under the windshield air-scoop.

All of the Honda ballast resistors can be tested in either of two ways.

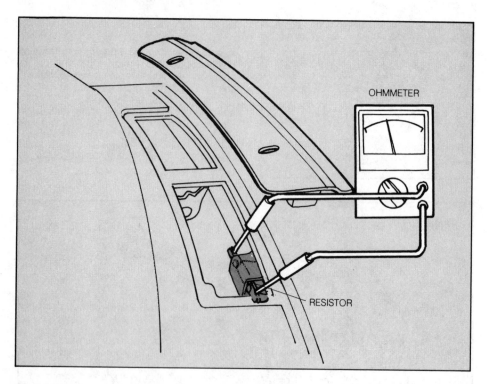

OHMMETER

RESISTOR

First test

1 Connect the terminal of the test light to a good ground.

2 Probe each terminal of the resistor with the key in the "on" position. If the test light doesn't light on both sides of the resistor, the resistor should be replaced.

Second test

1 Disconnect the ignition wires.

2 Connect an ohmmeter to each side of the resistor. The ohmmeter reading should be 1.6 ohms. If outside of specs, replace the resistor.

PRO SHOP The ignition coil transforms low battery voltage into high ignition voltage. While there is no prescribed maintenance for a coil, you can help keep it efficient by cleaning the tower of dirt while you are servicing the distributor. Inspect the top for electrical tracking between the center tower and the positive (+) and negative (−) terminals. Replace the coil if it is physically damaged or if there is evidence of tracking. Make sure the positive (+) and negative (−) wires are securely attached.

Check ignition coil

1 **Disconnect the coil wires** from their terminals and mark them for easy reinstallation.

2 **Connect one of the probes** of the ohmmeter to the battery positive (+) terminal and the other probe to the negative (−) terminal. The readings should be, with an ohmmeter on the low ohms (×1) scale, for 1973, 3.8 ohms; 1974–79 non-electronic ignition 1.5 ohms; electronic ignition 1979 Accords and Preludes 1.9 ohms; and all 1980 models 1.2 ohms.

3 **Switch from the low ohms (×1) scale** to the high ohms scale (×1000).

4 **On non-electronic ignition coils,** connect one probe to the large secondary tower and the other probe to the negative (−) terminal. These readings should be, for 1973, 8000 ohms and 1974–79 non-electronic ignition 10,000 ohms.

OR if your Honda has electronic ignition, connect one probe to the large secondary tower, but connect the other probe to the positive (+) primary terminal. These readings should be, for 1979 Accords and Preludes, 11,000 ohms and for all 1980 models 9200 ohms. All of these readings are ideal and some variation is acceptable. Also, these readings will vary with temperature. If any of these conditions is not met, the coil should be replaced.

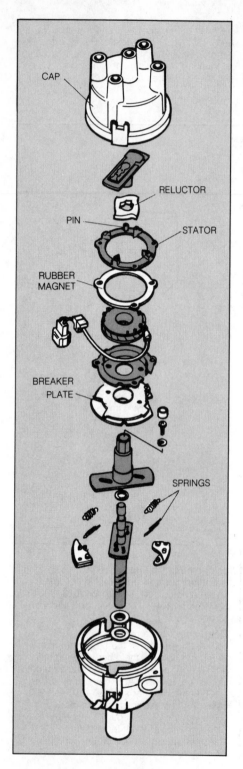

CAP

RELUCTOR

PIN

STATOR

RUBBER
MAGNET

BREAKER
PLATE

SPRINGS

All about electronic ignition systems

In an electronic ignition system, the points and condenser have been replaced by a non-mechanical triggering system, usually a reluctor and pickup assembly, installed where the breaker set would be in a conventional system. The primary voltage is no longer routed through a distributor, but through an electronic control unit where a switching transistor, activated by the reluctor and pickup, makes and breaks the primary circuit. Since there is no physical contact between the parts of the triggering system, only magnetic oscillations, parts do not wear out. The elimination of point wear has three advantages: greater output, increased reliability, and less service and maintenance.

Higher voltage output is necessary to fire the lean mixture in today's low-compression, emission-controlled engines. When working on the electronic ignition system in your car, keep in mind that it is possible for your system to develop up to 47,000 volts. This higher voltage has a wearing effect on the secondary components that is only partially offset by the use of new materials. When problems develop in your ignition system, such as increased resistance from worn spark plugs, the high voltage supplied can burn holes in the distributor cap and rotor. In cases of electronic ignition-system failure, however, it's usually something other than the cap or rotor that's to blame. And in every electronic ignition system, the spark plug cables can age before their time because of the high voltage and under-the-hood temperatures. So when you replace them, make sure you get the right ones, which are usually insulated with silicone.

The 1979 Accords (including LX- and 4-door models) and Preludes and all 1980 Hondas incorporate an electronic transistor ignition system. This is not to be confused with High Energy Ignition, although the available voltage is slightly higher than the earlier models with the conventional points and condenser ignition system.

Hondas use three different electronic ignition systems. However, the biggest difference is in the shape and location of the components in the system. For example, the 1979 and 1980 Accord and Prelude models have the igniter mounted on the firewall near the coil and the pulse generator mounted inside the distributor, whereas on the 1980 Civic models the igniter/pulse generator is a single unit mounted inside the distributor. The 1979 Accord and Prelude models use a four-pole stator inside the distributor. All 1980 models utilize a two-pole stator. All models with an electronic ignition system use a similar reluctor and rotor located inside the distributor.

Some do's and don'ts
- Don't do anything to cause a high voltage surge (connecting a jumper cable backwards, for example).
- Don't drive the car with a malfunctioning charging system.
- Don't allow stray sparks from loose wires.
- Don't ever hook up the battery cables backwards.
- Do make sure all wires and cables are properly hooked up.
- Do connect the tachometer negative (—) side of the coil.
- Do diagnose the problem as no spark to the plugs before considering the electronic ignition system at fault.

1 First test to see if spark is getting to the plugs. Follow the procedure outlined in the chapter on Spark Plug Service, testing for spark.

2 Test the ignition coil as outlined in this chapter. Note that the resistance is different for models with electronic ignition and also that these models do not use a ballast resistor.

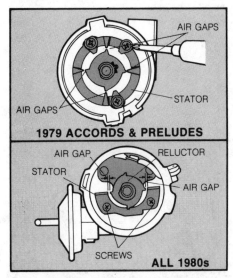

1979 ACCORDS & PRELUDES

ALL 1980s

3 Inspect the air gap between the stator and the reluctor. The gaps must be equal. The 1979 Accord and Prelude models have four gaps. All 1980 models have only two air gaps.

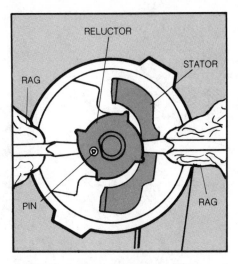

4 If the reluctor is to be removed, use care so you don't damage it. Pry it up carefully on both sides and be careful not to drop the small pin.

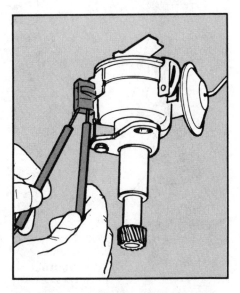

5 On 1979 and 1980 Accords (including the LX-and four-door models) and Preludes, test the pulse generator. Using an ohmmeter, test for a resistance of 600 to 800 ohms on the 1979 models and 800 to 1200 on the 1980 models. This reading may be slightly higher if the temperature is above 70°F, but should not exceed 1000 ohms on these models. Testing the 1980 Civic pulse generator/ignitor system should be performed by a professional.

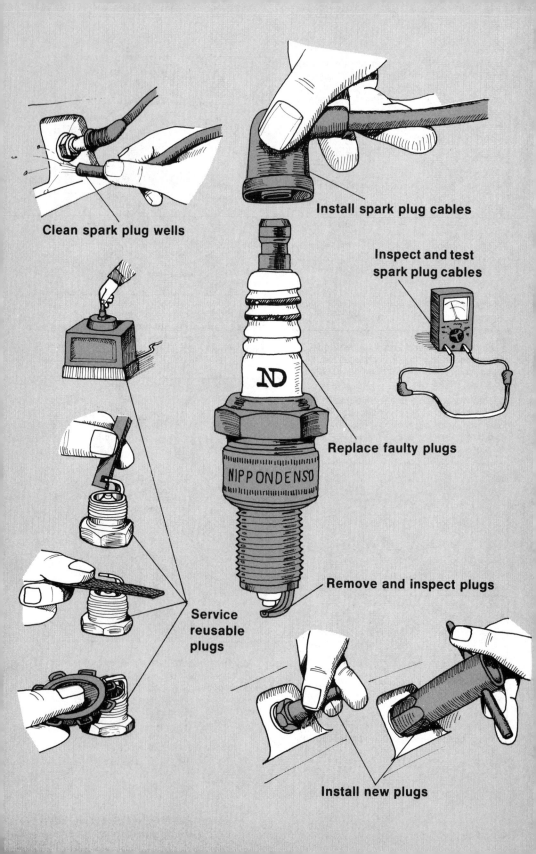

Clean spark plug wells

Install spark plug cables

Inspect and test spark plug cables

Replace faulty plugs

ND

NIPPONDENSO

Remove and inspect plugs

Service reusable plugs

Install new plugs

8

Spark Plug Service

1 Clean spark plugs wells. Cleaning the wells prevents dirt and sand particles from falling into them, which could cause extensive internal damage (p. 76).

2 Remove and inspect plugs. Check the plugs for cracks, compression leaks, electrode wear, and oil or carbon deposits (p. 76).

3 Service reusable plugs. Clean them with a wire brush or sandblaster plug cleaner. Open the plug gap and file the electrode square. Gap the plugs and reinstall them in the same spark plug holes (p. 80).

4 Replace faulty plugs. Make sure the new plugs have the same thread reach and seat design as the ones you removed. Also, be sure the new plugs meet your car's heat range and gap specs (p. 82).

5 Install new plugs. Screw in the plugs by hand until they are finger-tight. Then seat them to correct torque (p. 82).

6 Inspect and test spark plug cables. Check them for cuts, punctures, cracks, and age. Test them for resistance (p. 83). Damaged or old cables can mean poor engine performance and gas mileage, as well as hard starting in damp or wet weather.

7 Install spark plug cables. Make sure the cables are of the correct length and are routed properly (p. 84).

Essential. Basic tools • Spark plug socket, universal joint, extension, and ratchet • Spark plug cleaning solvent • Stiff brush • Ignition file • Wire feeler gauge • Towels or clean rags • Ohmmeter • Thread chaser.

Handy. Masking tape and/or spring clothespin • Spark plug cable remover (special insulated pliers) • Sandblaster (plug cleaner) • Electrode bending tool • Torque wrench.

ECONOTIP Various tests have been carried out by car manufacturers and the federal government to find out whether idling or restarting uses more fuel. Especially with today's frequent gas lines, the right practice may save some fuel. Depending on the study conducted, you should not idle more than half a minute, or a full minute. If the engine idles longer than that, it will take less gas to restart it than to keep it running. It's clear from the studies that anything longer than a minute is wasteful. But your engine may be one of those that should not idle over half a minute. In the long run, you will probably save the most gas by turning the engine off the second you enter a line. That is much better than leaving the engine running in the hope the line will move quickly and ending up with a total idle time of five minutes.

Clean spark plug wells

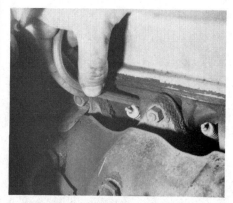

Plugs on the CVCC engine from 1975–80 are easily removed for cleaning of the wells. Clean them with a small stiff bristle brush. Also clean around the plugs to loosen and remove all dirt and sand.

The plugs on the Civic 1200s from 1973–79 are not as accessible, especially on the 1975–79 Civic 1200 models equipped with air pumps. On these cars you may want to use air to blow the dirt away.

Remove and inspect plugs

Before removing the spark plug wires, label each one, either with masking tape or a spring clothespin, so you will be able to connect the right cable to the proper plug after you have serviced all the plugs. All Hondas have an in-line 4-cylinder engine. This engine is transverse-mounted and the plug wires should be numbered from left-to-right. Left-to-right is determined by the driver's seat position, facing the engine compartment.

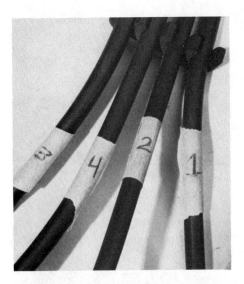

On the Civic 1200, the plug wires go through a bracket across the front.
On the CVCC engine, the plug wires run through a bracket from the back of the engine. Remember that the cables routed through the brackets on the cylinder head cover are not always in the same sequence as they appear attached to the plugs.

1 To remove the spark plug wires, grasp the boot, the heavy, rubbery part at the spark plug port, with a plug cable remover and twist it back and forth to free it from the plug. Then pull on the boot.

OR if you don't have a special wire remover, make sure the engine is cold, then grasp the cable by its boot and carefully twist it back and forth to free it from the plug terminal. Then, still holding the boot, pull it carefully off the plug. Remove all the cables this way.

🛑 If you try to remove the cables by pulling on the wires, you stand a good chance of breaking the electrical conductors inside, so always grab the cables by their boots.

🛑 Remember that all Hondas have aluminum heads. The spark plugs should be removed when the engine is cool. Also, since aluminum is softer than the cast iron sometimes used for heads, more care should be taken when removing or reinstalling spark plugs. Don't force the plug; work it out.

2 To remove the spark plugs, use a spark plug socket, a universal joint (if necessary), a short extension, and a ratchet. Place the socket over the plug and turn the wrench counterclockwise. The spark plug socket used on most cars is a standard $^{13}/_{16}$-inch hex (19 mm). If you plan to reuse the plugs, take care in removing them. Keep the wrench as straight as possible so you don't break the insulation.

Reading your plugs

Knowing how to "read" your plugs can help you do a better job tuning up your car. The 15 descriptions which follow should get you going:

1 Fluffy gray deposits: Normal for emmission-controlled engines and no-lead fuel. Plug has high mileage and should be replaced.

2 Soft deposits on center and darker deposits on side electrodes: proper heat range at moderate speeds.

3 Light tan deposits on a well-used plug.

4 Soft white deposits on center electrode and insulator; Normal for engine using fuel with metallic additives.

5 Normal fluffy brown deposits on insulator. Sooty deposits on shell suggest a rich mixture.

6 Slightly oily deposits on shell: Engine probably not fully broken in.

7 Detonation damage: Possible causes: a) over-advanced ignition timing; b) fuel too low in octane; c) EGR system malfunctioning.

8 Preignition damage: White deposits on insulator, burned electrodes: Possible causes: a) plug too hot; b) advanced ignition timing; c) cooling or exhaust system clogged.

9 Sooty deposits on insulator and electrodes: Possible causes: a) excessively rich mixture due to sticking choke or defective carburetor; b) faulty primary circuit or spark plug wires; c) starting without engine warmup.

10 Oil fouled: Possible causes: a) piston ring or valve-guide seal leakage; b) defective PCV system.

11 Carbon fouled: Possible causes: a) oil passing rings or valves; b) defective PCV system; c) spark plug too cold; d) incorrect plug.

12 Dirt fouling: Look for defective air cleaner.

13 Bridged gap: Deposits accumulated at low speed break loose at full power.

14 Glazed insulator: May mean spark plug too hot.

15 Splashed insulator: Oily accumulation in cylinder breaks loose and fouls plug after tuneup.

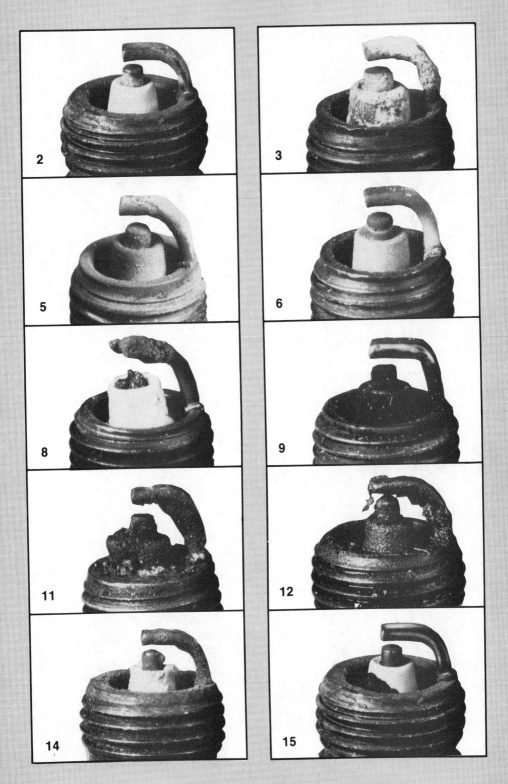

Inspect the tops as well as the tips

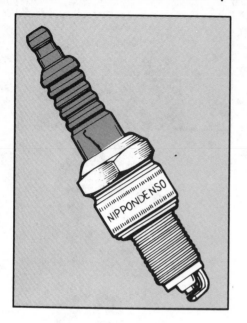

Check the condition of the electrodes. If the porcelain is cracked or scorched, the plug must be replaced. If the outer ground electrode is damaged, the plug is bad and the air gap can never be properly adjusted. If the gasket is cracked or the shell is damaged, the plug must be replaced.

Service reusable plugs

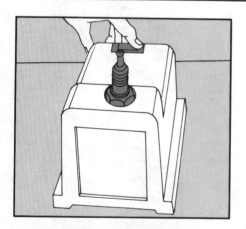

If the plugs appear to be OK, and they have been in the car for less than 10,000 miles, you can clean, file, regap, and reinstall them. If they don't show too much wear, you can simply wash them with a solvent and a stiff brush. Never use a wire brush on the electrodes as this may "etch" them, allowing fresh deposits to adhere more easily.

1 The best way to clean plugs is to sandblast them. If you don't have this kind of plug cleaner, for a small fee one of your local service shops will sandblast them. But don't think they're ready to be reinstalled in your car yet.

PRO SHOP As you remove the plugs, you will need a holder for them to prevent damage to the porcelain. You can use an egg carton, a drilled block of wood or a heavy piece of cardboard. It is a good idea to keep the plugs in the same order as the cylinders from which they were removed. When you examine the plugs, knowing the cylinder each one came from will help you pinpoint any engine problem you may find.

2 Carefully widen the electrode gap to permit proper filing of the center electrode. Sandblast cleaning not only removes the deposits but rounds off the electrodes as well, and it may remove certain essential alloys from them. So the center electrode must be filed vigorously until the tip is flat and the edges square and sharp.

3 Check the gap whether you are using cleaned plugs or new ones. Use a round (wire-type) feeler gauge to do this. On all Hondas (except 1980's with 1300 cc and 1500 cc engines), set the plug gap between 0.7 and 0.8 mm (.028 to .032 inches). 1980 models with 1300 cc and 1500 cc engines have a gap between 1.0 and 1.1 mm (.039 to .043 inches). Push the wire gauge into the gap and then pull it out. If there is a slight drag or friction between the wire and the gap surfaces, the gap is correct. If the gauge goes in easily or falls through, then the side (ground) electrode must be bent down toward the center electrode to narrow the gap. You should use a special bending tool for this.

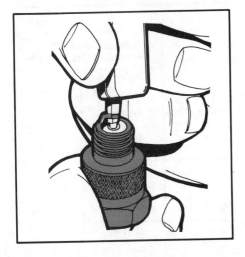

4 Recheck the gap and repeat the bending process until you get the correct gap.

5 If you cannot push the gauge into the gap, then it is too narrow and the side electrode must be bent up from the center electrode. Don't worry if you don't get it right the first time. Even the pros have to bend the electrode several times before getting the correct gap.

Replace faulty plugs

When replacing spark plugs, make sure you buy the right ones. Know the thread diameter of the plugs used in your car. The two most popular today are 14 mm and 18 mm. Some plugs have a tapered seat design, while others use a gasket. All Hondas use the gasket-style and have a thread diameter of 14 mm.

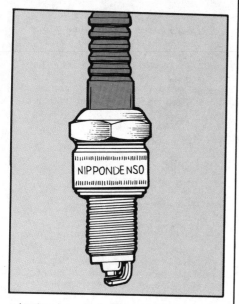

Another important factor is thread reach. Spark plugs have different thread reaches, depending on the manufacturer. The thread reach is the distance from the shell seat to the end of the threaded section. Some plugs are designated long-reach, others short-reach. It is important for proper combustion to make sure you install plugs that have the same thread reach and the same seat design as the ones removed from your engine. Again, all Hondas use the same reach, that is 19 mm (¾-inches). It is best to install the same type of plug as came with the car originally. If you are in doubt as to the right plugs, consult your owner's manual or the under-the-hood label. When installing new plugs, never use short-reach plugs in a long-reach cylinder head. If you do, it will reduce combustion efficiency and increase your engine's fuel consumption. It can also severely damage the engine.

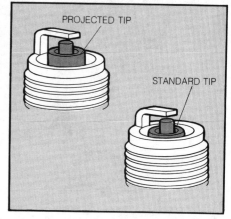

One of the most important differences in the spark plugs used in Hondas is the structure; there is a standard-tip design and a projected-tip design. The Civic 1200 from 1973–79 use the projected-tip design while all the CVCC Hondas use the standard-tip design.

Install new plugs

1 Make sure the plug seat and thread area are clean and free of dirt. Run a thread chaser through the cylinder head threads to ease installation of the plugs.

2 Place new gaskets over the plug threads if you're reinstalling the original plugs.

3 Screw the plugs in by hand until they are finger-tight. The Honda uses the gasket-type plug and it should be tightened one-quarter turn more if you don't have a torque wrench. If you have one, torque to 14 foot pounds.

Spark Plug Thread Size Gasket Type	RECOMMENDED INSTALLATION TORQUE	
	Aluminum Heads With Torque Wrench After Seating	Without Torque Wrench After Seating
10 mm	8–12 lb./ft.	¼ turn
12 mm	10–16	¼ turn
*14 mm	12–18	¼ turn
18 mm	14–	¼ turn

* All Hondas 1973–1980

Go chase a thread

This is a thread chaser and seat-cleaning tool, and you can and should buy one from your auto parts dealer if you do your own spark plug work. Its job is to thoroughly clean the threads and seats before the plugs are installed and it's worth every cent you spend for it.

STOP If you fail just once to clean the seat of a spark plug port properly, a particle can lodge between the plug shell and the cylinder head. The outcome, at the least, could be a ruined plug. At the most, the cylinder head can be destroyed. Use extreme care with the Honda because all the heads are aluminum and softer than cast iron heads.

Spark plug heat ranges

The term heat range refers to a plug's ability to dissipate the heat from the combustion chamber into nearby water jackets in the cylinder head. To achieve maximum engine performance under different driving conditions, spark plugs have various operating temperatures or heat ranges.

The range is determined by the length of the insulator and how fast the plug can transfer heat from the insulator and electrodes into the cooling system and the atmosphere. The shorter the insulator tip, the colder the plug. The heat range is designated by a number on the porcelain. On original-equipment Honda plugs, the higher the number, the colder the plug. The heat range of a plug has nothing to do with its ability to fire the fuel-and-air mixture. It simply states that a cold plug will transfer heat away from the tip more rapidly than a hot plug.

Inspect and test plug cables

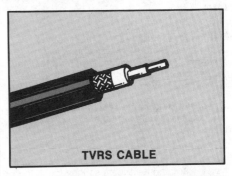

TVRS CABLE

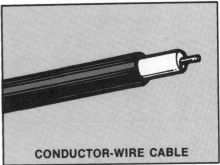

CONDUCTOR-WIRE CABLE

Suppression-type cables, known as TVRS (Television-Radio Supressor) are standard equipment today because they prevent radio and television interference. But you may also find conductor wire (metal core) cables on older Hondas. If your car has this kind of cable, replace it with the suppression-type.

1 Inspect the cables for cracks, burns, oil, and grease. Bend them and check for brittleness or deterioration. If a cable fails the inspection, replace the entire set of cables, not just one or two.

2 To test plug cable resistance, remove one cable at a time from the spark plug and the distributor cap.

3 Connect an ohmmeter between the ends of the cable. If the ohmmeter leads are probe types, you can insert them so they touch the terminals. Make sure they make good contact. If your ohmmeter has alligator clips, you can make contact with the spark plug end of the cable by inserting a screwdriver into the boot and attaching the alligator clip to the shank of the screwdriver.

4 If resistance is more than 25,000 ohms, you should replace the cables.

STOP Don't touch the metal part of the probes while taking your resistance reading because your body will add a certain amount of resistance.

5 Test the cables for breaks. Sometimes spark plug cables have breaks that are not visible to the naked eye. To test them, attach one end of a jumper wire to a screwdriver blade and the other end to a good ground.

6 Disconnect a cable from its plug. The engine should be running for this test. Hold the plug cable away from the engine and make sure it doesn't arc (ground).

7 Pass the screwdriver blade along the length of the cable. If sparking occurs, it means there's a break in that cable and it should be replaced.

8 Test the other plug cables in the same way.

Install spark plug cables

1 Avoiding cable mix-up is the trick here. Remove the longest cable first. On a CVCC engine, that is the cable from the number 1 cylinder. On the Civic 1200 engine, the longest cable is number 4. Disconnect the same cable from the distributor cap tower and lay it aside.

2 Pick a new cable about the same length as the one just removed (it can be slightly longer). Install this new cable, first in the distributor cap and then onto the spark plug. Do this for each of the cables, making sure the cables are firmly attached.

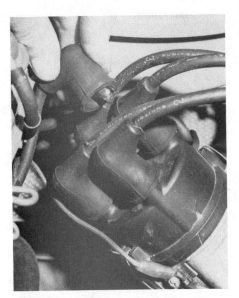

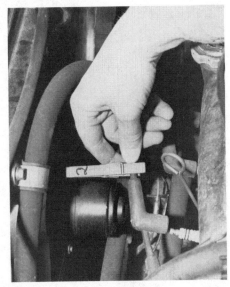

3 When removing the old cable from the distributor, inspect the cap for corrosion or damage. If you find such a condition, correct the problem before hooking up the other cables.

🛑 When arranging plug cables, be sure the new ones are not resting on any moving parts or on any hot engine parts. Also try to keep the hoses from resting on the cables. If the cables were in a clip or harness, put the new ones back in the same way.

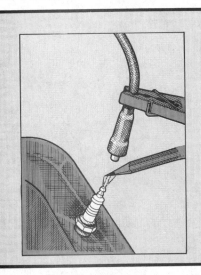

Plugs, pencils, and polarity

When you replace a coil, make sure the two primary leads are reconnected properly. A reverse connection reverses polarity, considerably decreasing the voltage available for ignition. An easy way to check polarity is to disconnect any cable at the spark plug and insert the tip of a soft lead pencil between the cable and the plug while the engine is running. The spark flare will be toward the plug terminal if the polarity is right. If not, reverse the leads at the coil.

ECONOTIP If you have ever watched a jackrabbit start running, you know they get up to full speed almost instantly. Jackrabbits are built for fast starts, high speed, and quick turns. The modern passenger car is not. Trying to imitate a jackrabbit when starting from a dead stop can use 15 percent more gas. The best mileage comes from gradual acceleration.

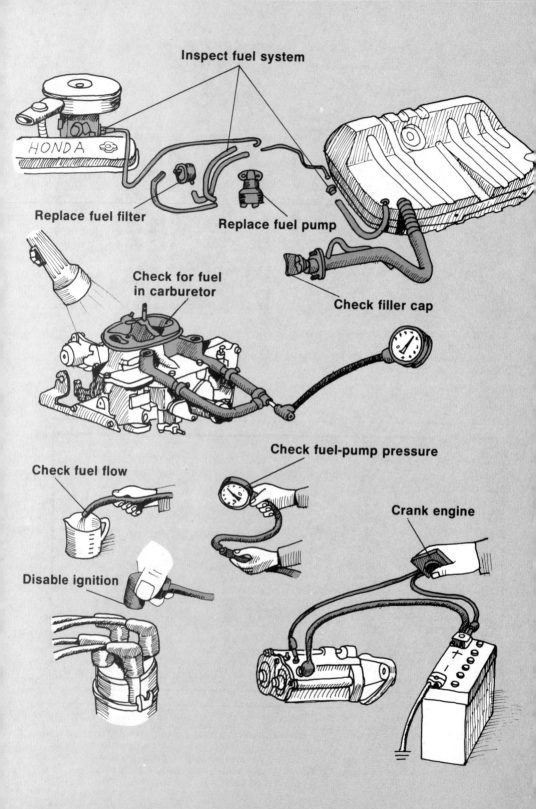

Inspect fuel system

HONDA

Replace fuel filter

Replace fuel pump

Check for fuel in carburetor

Check filler cap

Check fuel-pump pressure

Check fuel flow

Crank engine

Disable ignition

9

Fuel System Service

1 Inspect fuel system. Carefully check the system for leaks by starting at the carburetor inlet and tracing the fuel lines all the way back to the fuel tank. If there are any leaks or damaged lines, repair or replace them as necessary (p.88).

2 Check for fuel in carburetor. Remove the top of the air cleaner and shine a flashlight into the carburetor while opening and closing the throttle. There should be a small stream of gasoline each time the throttle is opened. Make sure the accelerator pump is working (p.89).

3 Check filler cap. A fuel smell inside the car can be caused by an improperly seated or defective cap (p.90).

4 Disable ignition. To prevent the engine from starting, remove the coil wire from the center of the distributor cap and ground with a jumper wire (p.90).

5 Crank engine. If you don't have a helper to crank the engine from inside the car, you'll need a remote starter switch (p.91).

6 Check fuel flow. This tells you if gasoline is flowing freely from the tank through the fuel pump to the carburetor. Disconnect the fuel line at the carburetor inlet and crank the engine (p.91).

7 Check fuel-pump pressure. This tells you if the fuel system is capable of providing enough fuel to the engine for all operating conditions (p.92).

8 Replace fuel pump. If the flow or pressure tests indicate a defective pump, you should replace it (p.92).

9 Replace fuel filter. Honda fuel filters are transparent and if you find dirt or sediment, the filter should be replaced (p.95).

Essential. Basic tools • Class B-type fire extinguisher • Flashlight • Cutting pliers •

Towels or clean rags • Test light • Vacuum/pressure gauge • Safety fuel can.
Handy. Fender cover • Remote starter switch • Tubing flaring tool • Masking tape • Floor jack • Support stands • Drain pan.

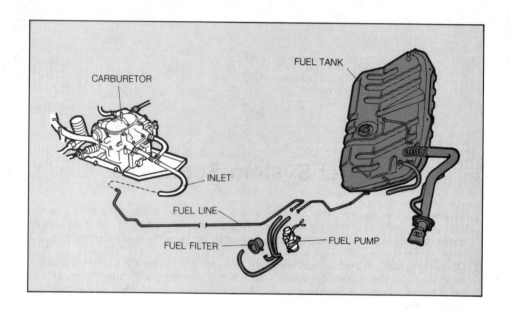

Inspect fuel system

The fuel system is not complex but it carries gasoline. *CAUTION: Gasoline and gas vapors are more dangerous and explosive than dynamite. Exercise extreme care when working with the fuel system. In order to ensure the safe operation of your car, you should check the fuel system for any potentially dangerous situations. You do not have to have a puddle of gas to have a dangerous situation. Gas vapors are more dangerous and because they are heavier than air, they settle down. Do not create any sparks while working with the fuel system, wipe up any spilled gasoline at once, and work only in a well-ventilated area.*

Inspect for fuel leaks by starting at the carburetor inlet. Trace the fuel lines back, into the car, then out of the inside of the car, to the fuel pump, the fuel filter, and then to the fuel tank.

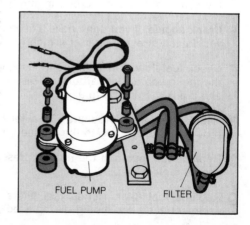

To replace fuel lines

Damaged fuel lines must be replaced with ones similar in construction to the original. A steel line must be replaced with a steel line, a neoprene line with a neoprene line. In some cases, it may be necessary to jack up and support the rear of the car to gain access to the lines.

Replace flexible fuel lines at gas tank

1 Jack up and support the rear of the car. Use a flashlight rather than a droplight (there is less chance of spark).

2 Remove the clamps which hold the flexible fuel line to the fuel tank outlet and the steel fuel line with the correct tool.

3 Place a drain pan under the line to catch any fuel spilled when you separate the connection.

4 Now remove the flexible line by twisting and pulling it off of the fuel tank outlet and the steel line.

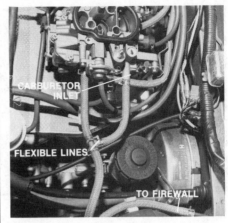

5 Install the new flexible line on the fuel tank outlet and the steel line, then reinstall the clamps.

🛑 Use care when replacing the flexible lines between the steel tubing at the firewall and the carburetor. Remember to use the drain pan and properly reposition the clamps after installation of the flexible hose.

Check for fuel in carburetor

This test and others to follow may be more easily accomplished if you remove the air-cleaner top and use masking tape to label all the hoses you remove for easier reinstallation.

1 Shine a flashlight into the throat of the carburetor. The choke should be open and the engine off.

2 Open and close the throttle three times or have a helper pump the gas pedal. If there is a small squirt of gasoline each time the

throttle is opened, then gasoline is reaching the carburetor. If you are troubleshooting a no-start condition, your problem is elsewhere and further investigation of the fuel system is not required. If there isn't any gasoline squirting into the carburetor, proceed to the next step.

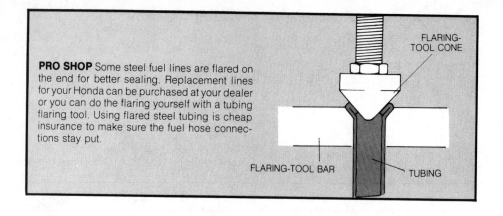

PRO SHOP Some steel fuel lines are flared on the end for better sealing. Replacement lines for your Honda can be purchased at your dealer or you can do the flaring yourself with a tubing flaring tool. Using flared steel tubing is cheap insurance to make sure the fuel hose connections stay put.

FLARING-TOOL CONE

FLARING-TOOL BAR

TUBING

Check filler cap

All Hondas use a vacuum pressure filler cap. This allows the gas vapors in the tank to be vented through the charcoal canister rather than into the atmosphere. These caps only vent to the air when the pressure in the tank exceeds about two and a half psi. A strong gas smell can mean faulty pressure relief or poor sealing between the cap and the filler neck. If you suspect this, replace the cap. Seldom will a failed gas cap cause a no-start condition on a Honda. But, if you remove the cap on a no-start car and it now starts, you should have it further tested by a professional mechanic.

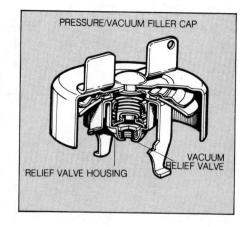

PRESSURE/VACUUM FILLER CAP

RELIEF VALVE HOUSING

VACUUM RELIEF VALVE

Disable ignition

1 To prevent the engine from starting, remove the coil high tension wire from the distributor center tower.

2 Using a jumper wire, ground the coil wire as outlined in the chapter on Starting System Service.

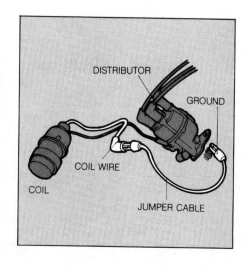

DISTRIBUTOR

GROUND

COIL WIRE

COIL

JUMPER CABLE

ECONOTIP The 55 MPH speed limit saves gas, but it takes longer to get where you are going. How much longer was answered a few years ago by Buick Division of General Motors. They ran several cars from San Diego, California, to Washington, D.C. One group of cars ran at 50 MPH, while the other group ran at 70. This was before the 55 MPH limit was enacted. The 50 MPH group took 14 hours longer to cross the country than the 70 MPH group, but they used 22.9 percent less gasoline than the faster cars. It was not reported how much more the slower group spent on motel bills and meals during the extra time they were on the road. Since the savings of gas amounted to about one tankful, it probably did not equal the extra spent for meals and gas. So 55 MPH saves gas, wear on the car, and maybe your life, but it obviously increases the cost of a long trip.

Crank engine

Have a helper crank the engine from inside the car if possible. You can hook up a remote starter switch between the battery and the starter solenoid as detailed in the chapter on Starting System Service. But because of the danger involved in working with gasoline, it is safer if you have both hands free. And make sure your helper knows where the fire extinguisher is located.

Check fuel flow

This test will tell you if gasoline is flowing freely from the fuel tank to the carburetor.

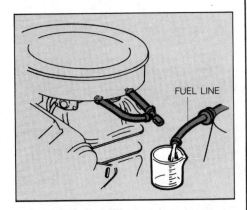

FUEL LINE

1 Disconnect the fuel line at the carburetor inlet, at the carburetor on the Civic 1200, and just before the tee going to the carburetor on CVCC engines.

2 Attach a rubber hose to the end of the line.

3 Place the hose in a measuring instrument (preferably not glass).

4 Crank the engine for 20 seconds. A pulsing stream of fuel means the fuel pump is supplying fuel to the carburetor. You should get a measured amount of about four and one-half ounces from the Civic 1200 between 1973 and 1979 and from 1975–79 CVCC sedans and wagons, and a measured five ounces from 1976–78 Accords and 1980 Civics. If the measured amounts for 20 seconds are not within specs and there is only a trickle of fuel or no fuel at all, it means you have a defective fuel pump or a blocked line between the fuel tank and the carburetor. Blocked fuel lines are unlikely unless the car has been in an accident or the fuel filter is blocked.

5 Check fuel pump pressure just to verify that the pump is OK, even if you get the correct measured amounts of fuel.

Check fuel pump

To isolate the fuel pump as the defective component on Civic 1200's from 1973–79, check fuel pump pressure.

If you have a Honda equipped with the CVCC engine from 1975–80, keep in mind that this model has an electrical fuel pump. So a blown fuse could be the cause of a no-start condition. If the main fuse (in the engine compartment) and the fuel pump fuse in the fuse box check OK, then the relay or other electrical connections may be the problem. Have the car further tested by a professional mechanic. If the electrical connections are OK and there is an audible ticking sound back by the fuel pump, proceed to the next check.

Check fuel-pump pressure

This tells you if the fuel pump is capable of providing enough fuel for the engine. The test is performed with a vacuum/pressure gauge which is connected to the hose you removed for the fuel flow check.

1 Crank the engine until it reaches its highest reading. On all Hondas from 1973–80, the fuel-pump pressure reading should be between two and three psi. If pressure is less than two psi, you probably have a defective pump.

2 Make sure the fuel lines are open. The pump cannot draw gasoline from the tank if the line is blocked, crushed or kinked. If the lines are OK, you will have to replace the pump.

OR if on the CVCC no reading is obtained, there may be an electrical problem. See the

discussion in the fuel-flow check step. Also, if the fuel filter has just recently been replaced, one of the hoses may be kinked because of the tight location of the filter.

Replace fuel pump

1973 to 1979 Civic 1200's

The fuel pump on the 1973 to 1979 Civic 1200 is bolted to the cylinder head. Before you start removing it, take some safety precautions. Put a drain pan under the area of the fuel pump and remove the gas cap to release any pressure in the pump inlet line.

1 Disconnect the fuel inlet and outlet lines.

2 Plug the end of the inlet line to prevent unnecessary fuel leakage.

3 Remove the two nuts holding the pump to the head, then remove the pump.

4 Remove the old gasket, noting the way it came off since it can be reinstalled the wrong way.

5 Remove the insulator block.

6 Reinstall the block and new gasket.

7 Install the new pump, making sure the number 1 cylinder is on top dead center (note the timing mark) so the eccentric for the pump is turned away.

8 Unplug the inlet line and reconnect the inlet and outlet lines.

This is a mechanical fuel pump found on 1973–79 Civic 1200s. It is driven by an eccentric on the camshaft, located up in the head.

This is an electric fuel pump found on 1975–79 CVCC sedans and wagons, 1976–80 Accords, 1979–80 Preludes, and all 1980 Civics. It is located near the fuel tank. Electric fuel pumps receive voltage through a safety circuit that shuts the pump off when the engine stops, even if the ignition key is not turned off. This safety circuit is routed through the oil pressure switch—when the oil pressure drops, the pump is shut off. Before replacing an electric fuel pump that has failed the pressure test (p. 92), first inspect the electrical supply circuit. Use a test light and test for ground and voltage at the pump.

1975 to 1979 CVCC sedans

On 1975–79 CVCC sedans, the fuel pump is located in a covered well under the rear seat.

1 Remove the rear seat by removing a ten-mm bolt in the center at the rear of the seat.

2 Remove the two screws on the driver's side and loosen the other two screws that hold the cover for the pump well.

3 Remove the gas cap.

STOP Take care not to spill any gas. The smell will remain in the car.

4 Remove the three retaining bolts and unhook the electrical connection.

5 Lift the pump and carefully remove the two hoses.

6 Reverse the above procedure to install the new pump, making sure the spacer and bushing are in place. Be very careful not to kink the hoses as you are installing the pump.

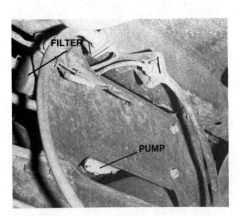

FILTER

PUMP

1975 to 1980 Wagons

On 1975–80 wagons, the fuel pump is located under the car behind the fuel tank.

1 Jack up the rear of the car and support it with safety stands.

2 Remove the gas cap, following all safety precautions.

3 Remove the fuel pump mounting bracket from behind the gas tank.

4 Disconnect the two fuel lines. Have something handy to use as a plug to keep gas from dripping. Now follow the removal and reinstallation procedures outlined for sedans.

ECONOTIP The next time your car needs tires, consider buying radials. They have considerably less rolling resistance than bias ply tires. You can actually feel this if you ever have occasion to push a car a few feet by hand. The bias ply tires make it difficult or almost impossible to get the car moving. Radials make even the heaviest car easy to push. The usual improvement in mileage is about three percent. The only disadvantage to radials is their somewhat harsher ride. The shock of hitting tar strips or pavement ridges is not absorbed by a radial tire. But this is a small penalty to pay for the better mileage.

1976 to 1980 Accords

On the 1976–80 Accords, the fuel pump is located under the car on a mounting bracket up behind the left rear tire.

1 Jack up the rear of the car and support it with safety stands.

2 Remove the gas cap.

3 Remove the four bolts holding the fuel pump platform.

4 Disconnect the two electrical wires then remove the inlet and outlet hoses carefully and plug them to prevent unnecessary fuel leakage.

5 Move the entire assembly to a work bench.

6 Remove the pump from the bracket.

7 Reverse the above procedures to install the new fuel pump.

1980 Civic

FUEL TANK

TRAILING ARM

FUEL PUMP

The 1980 Civic fuel pump is located in the same place as that of the Prelude (on the driver's side of the fuel tank and forward). The Civic fuel pump is not completely enclosed, but is on a small platform.

1 Jack up and support the car.

2 Remove the gas cap and electrical connector.

3 Remove the two fuel lines from the bottom of the pump itself.

4 To install the new pump, follow the same procedures as for the Accord models.

CAUTION: Remember gasoline is very dangerous. Do not smoke or cause sparks. Work in a well-ventilated area and use a flashlight instead of a droplight.

1979 and 1980 Preludes

1 Jack up the rear of the car and support it with safety stands. The fuel pump on the Prelude is completely enclosed in a metal case located on the driver's side of the fuel tank.

2 Remove the gas cap.

3 Unhook the electrical connection.

4 Disconnect the hose from its connection in the wheel well and then from the fuel filter.

5 To install the new pump, follow the same procedures as with the Accord models.

Replace fuel filter

FUEL FILTER

The fuel filter should be replaced any time the fuel pump is replaced, in accordance with the manufacturer maintenance requirements, or, if on visual observation, you notice that it is contaminated.

On all CVCC models the fuel filter is right next to and on the same bracket as the fuel pump, except for the Prelude and the 1980 Civics, on which the filter is mounted a few inches away on the fuel tank. On Civic 1200 models from 1973–79, the fuel filter is located on the firewall almost directly behind the car-buretor. To inspect or replace the filter, refer to the previous section on fuel pumps for the exact location of the filter on your particular model.

To remove any Honda fuel filter, remove the gas cap, remove the fuel-hose clamps, and twist the hoses from the filter. Reverse the procedure to install the new filter.

For fuel filter replacement on most models, it will be necessary to jack up the car and support it with safety stands.

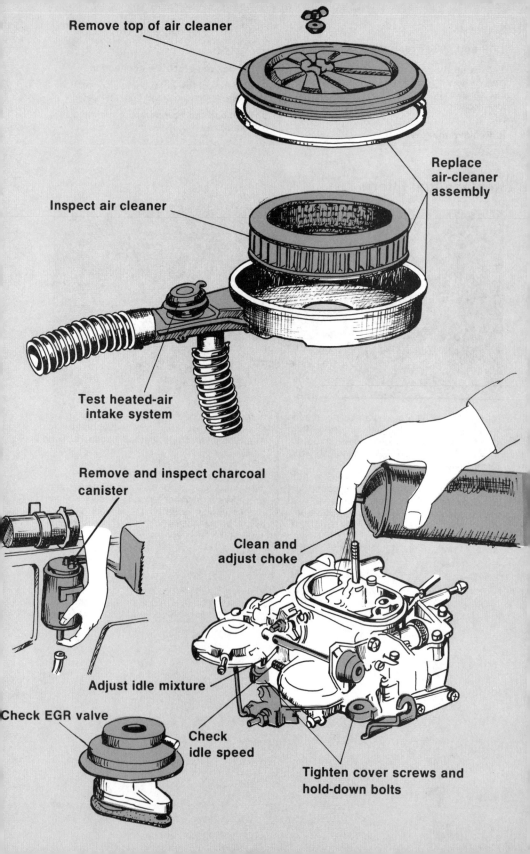

Remove top of air cleaner

Replace air-cleaner assembly

Inspect air cleaner

Test heated-air intake system

Remove and inspect charcoal canister

Clean and adjust choke

Adjust idle mixture

Check idle speed

Check EGR valve

Tighten cover screws and hold-down bolts

10

Carburetor Service

1 **Remove top of air cleaner.** Air cleaners are held on by a wing nut and spring clips. Inspect the condensation chamber (part of the Honda crankcase ventilation system) and the hoses. Clean or replace if necessary (p. 98).

2 **Test heated-air intake system.** Make sure the heated-air intake system is working properly. Start the engine. The flapper door should be closed (up) on a cold engine and open (down) on a warm engine. If it is not, check for binding linkage. Inspect the vacuum supply lines for cracks, leaks or restrictions. Check the vacuum motor and the heat-sensing valve (p. 99). Shut off the engine.

3 **Inspect air cleaner.** Disconnect the breather hose from the air cleaner at the valve cover. Remove the flexible fresh-air duct attached to the snorkel. Remove the hot-air tube from the underside of the snorkel. Tag and remove the vacuum hoses. Remove the attaching nuts and bolts. Lift the air-cleaner case off the carburetor and clean it (p. 101).

4 **Clean and adjust choke.** The choke should be closed when the engine is cold and open when it is warm (p. 101).

5 **Tighten cover screws and hold-down bolts.** The bolts should be snug (p. 102).

6 **Check EGR valve.** The EGR (exhaust gas recirculation) valve only appears on a few 1980 model Hondas and is operated by a complex set of controls. It should not be disconnected. If you suspect the EGR system is faulty, have it tested by a professional mechanic (p. 103).

7 **Remove and inspect charcoal canister.** Visually inspect the canister and replace if necessary (p. 103).

8 **Check idle speed.** Attach a tachometer to the engine. First set the curb-idle speed, then the fast-idle speed (p. 104).

9 **Adjust idle mixture.** All Hondas originally came with limiter caps on the mixture-adjusting screw to comply with emission laws. If adjusting this screw does not improve engine performance, the carburetor should be rebuilt or replaced (p. 106).

10 **Replace air-cleaner assembly.** Reattach all vacuum lines and hoses and reinstall the air filter (p. 107).

Essential. Basic tools • Tachometer • Flashlight • Vacuum gauge • Wheel chocks. **Handy.** Hose-clamp pliers • Fender cover • Vacuum pump • Masking tape.

Remove top of air cleaner

The air-cleaner top is held onto the carburetor by a wing nut and to the case by spring clips.

1 Turn the wing nut counterclockwise, then snap off the spring clips and remove the top. Be sure the engine is off.

2 Remove the air filter and set it aside.

3 Check the hose that goes from the valve cover to the condensation chamber (a small, light-gray chamber hanging down from the air-cleaner case). It should be free of cracks, kinks or restrictions.

4 Clean or replace the air cleaner if necessary.

Servicing carburetor air cleaner

You think you know everything you need to know about the carburetor air cleaner just because you change the filter frequently? True, a dirty filter has a choking effect on the engine that consumes fuel and, in time, leads to starting problems. But did you know that the whole air-cleaner assembly, which is usually taken off, set aside and forgotten during an inspection, could be the source of many problems?

Under certain conditions, different components of the air-cleaner assembly can fail and cause such problems as poor fuel economy, poor driveability with a cold or hot engine, cold weather carburetor icing, lack of power, and detonation. Also, that innocent-looking gasket between the air-cleaner housing and the carburetor air horn (part of the case on most Hondas), or the

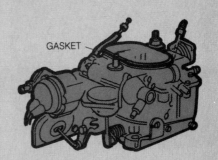

gasket between the case and the cover, can harm the engine if damaged. If either gasket is cracked or missing, dirt is drawn into the engine. So next time you change the filter, check those gaskets.

Test heated-air intake system

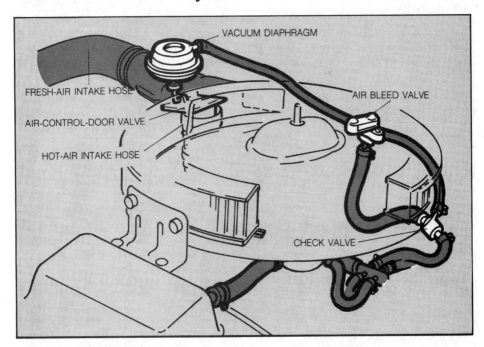

All Hondas from 1973–80 are equipped with a heated-air intake system to provide preheated air to the carburetor during cold engine warm-up and running. Air is passed over the exhaust manifold to warm it and then into the air-cleaner snorkel. A flapper valve (or door) in the snorkel controls the flow of air.

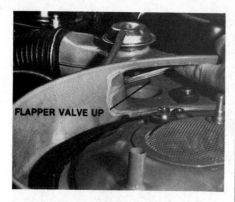

FLAPPER VALVE UP

FLAPPER VALVE DOWN

1 Start your engine when it is cold and let it idle.

2 Shine a flashlight into the snorkel (looking from the inside) and make sure the flapper valve (hot-air door) is in the warm-air or up position. The flapper valve on the Honda is vacuum-activated and if the valve fails to rise up on a cold engine, further testing is required.

3 Make sure the valve moves to the fresh-air position as the engine warms so that air is no longer drawn over the exhaust manifold into the snorkel. To check this you must reinstall the air-cleaner top until the engine cooling fan goes on because the sensor is in the air-cleaner case.

Troubleshooting heated-air intake system

The heated-air intake system is important in both cold and hot engine operation. If the flapper door fails to come up with the engine cold, check to see if it is binding in the air-cleaner housing. Also check the vacuum supply lines by starting at the vacuum motor mounted on the snorkel and working back to the source of vacuum. The motor is controlled by an air-bleed valve in the air-cleaner case. There should be vacuum to the motor and to the carburetor side of the air-bleed valve with the engine cold and running. You can check this with a vacuum gauge. If you have vacuum to the vacuum motor and the flapper valve still doesn't work, do the following:

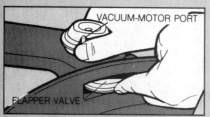

VACUUM-MOTOR PORT

FLAPPER VALVE

1 With the hose disconnected, manually lift the flapper valve.
2 Block the port on the vacuum motor.
3 Release the flapper valve. If the door closes, replace the vacuum motor. If the door remains up, replace the air-bleed valve.
4 Reconnect the hoses.

When the engine warms, the flapper valve should drop down, allowing fresh air to enter the air cleaner. This prevents super-heated air from entering the carburetor and causing such hot engine driving problems as surging, lack of power, and spark knock. Now, with the engine warm and running:

1 Remove the air-cleaner top.
2 Check immediately to see that the door drops. If it does, the system when the engine is hot is OK. If the door fails to drop, replace the air-bleed valve. But first, keep in mind that during normal driving, the valve rises and falls many times. So recheck in case you were in a normal down mode of operation.
3 Shut off the engine.

Inspect air cleaner

The air filter keeps dirt out of the carburetor and the element gradually fills up with dirt. If the filter isn't changed according to the manufacturer's recommended intervals, the carburetor will starve for air and hence waste gas.

1 Hold the filter up to the sky or examine it with a droplight. If you can see light through it and there aren't any holes or tears in the pleated-paper element, the filter can be reused.

2 Clean it by blowing, from the inside out, with compressed air, if available, or gently tap the filter on a flat surface to dislodge the particles. If the filter is clogged with dirt, damaged or wet with oil, replace it.

3 To remove the bottom part of the air-cleaner assembly, disconnect the breather hose at the valve cover.

4 Remove the fresh-air duct, the hot-air tube, and the attaching bolts (1980 models have several nuts inside the case which must also be removed).

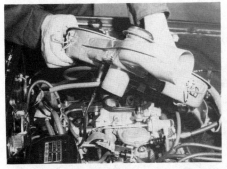

5 Gently lift the assembly up to see what vacuum hoses are attached to the underside.

6 Label the hoses with masking tape and remove them from their source.

7 Clean the air-cleaner case and reinstall it.

Clean and adjust choke

The choke limits the amount of air entering the carburetor when the engine is cold. If it doesn't close far enough, the engine will hestitate and stall when running. In extreme cases, it will fail to start altogether. The choke is preset at the factory and the only maintenance usually required is cleaning. The choke plate is the valve at the top of the carburetor.

Honda manual-choke cars

All Hondas before 1978 used manual chokes, which are operated by a choke knob on the dash. This representative choke mechanism was used on Civic 1200's from 1973–79.

This typical choke mechanism was used on 1975–79 CVCC sedans and wagons and on 1976–77 Accords.

Basic adjustment of manual chokes

Check the valve to see if it moves freely back and forth. If in doubt, spray some carburetor cleaner on the pivot points at the side of the carburetor. The choke also activates a fast-idle cam. This increases idle speed by holding the throttle open farther than it is when the engine is warm and the choke knob pushed in. While cleaning the choke, spray the carburetor around the fast-idle cam. The cam should now pivot freely.

On Civic models from 1973–79, with the choke knob pushed all the way in, the choke butterfly valve should be completely open. With the knob pulled out, the valve should be closed. If either condition is not met, adjust the cable length at the carburetor.

On CVCC models with manual chokes, with the choke knob pushed all the way in, the choke valve should again be completely open. When you pull the choke knob out to the second detent position, the valve should just close. With the knob pulled further out, the valve position should not change. If it does, adjust the cable length at the carburetor.

Honda automatic-choke cars

The automatic-choke mechanism is found on 1978 Accords (LX and 4-door models), 1979 Preludes, and all 1980 Hondas. Automatic chokes are activated by a bimetal spring attached to the side of the carburetor. With the engine cold, the choke should snap shut (at least within an eighth of an inch) when the accelerator is opened. Make sure the choke valve and associated linkage moves freely. You can spray them with some carburetor cleaner. The automatic choke on the Honda has an electrically assisted choke warm-up with several electrical components.

Both manual- and automatic-choke carburetors have a vacuum assembly which opens the choke plate slightly when the engine is started. The vacuum pulloff is activated by engine vacuum. If this pulloff diaphragm or the automatic choke is not operating, they should be further tested by a professional mechanic.

Tighten cover screws and hold-down bolts

HOLD-DOWN NUT

Sometimes a carburetor can work its way loose due to the vibrations created by a running engine. Check the screws around the top of the carburetor and the bolts around the base that holds the carburetor to the manifold. They should be torqued, but if you don't have a torque wrench, make sure the bolts are snug.

Check EGR valve

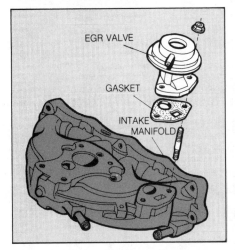

1980 is the first year Honda has installed an exhaust gas recirculation (EGR) valve and it appears on a few models. The EGR valve should be checked after the first 60,000 miles. On the Honda, the EGR valve only opens when the engine is hot and then only during acceleration above 20 MPH and while cruising (times when it should not affect performance). EGR valves are operated by a complex set of controls and you should not disconnect them. If you suspect a faulty valve, have it tested by a professional mechanic.

Remove and inspect charcoal canister

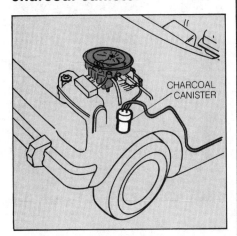

As part of the emission control system, the charcoal canister stores gasoline vapors that, prior to the establishment of emission control standards, were vented to the atmosphere. The vapors stored in the canister are drawn into the engine when it is running. The charcoal canister is located on the firewall or left-side fender well. The Honda charcoal canister does not have a replaceable filter in the bottom, so the canister should be inspected, checked, and replaced at recommended intervals.

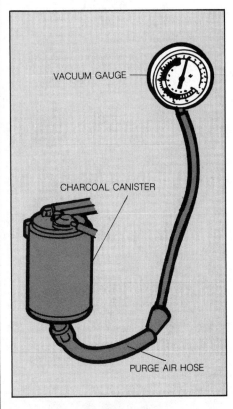

1 **Visually inspect the canister** for cracks.

2 **Inspect the hoses** going to the canister for cracks or kinks.

3 **Connect all the hoses on the top** and adapt a very sensitive vacuum gauge (if possible, one graduated in tenths of an inch).

4 **Connect a tachometer.**

5 **Start up a warmed engine** and run at 4000 rpm's for one minute.

6 **Observe the vacuum gauge** very closely. If you get a vacuum reading, more than one inch for 1973–77 Hondas and perhaps less than one inch for 1978–80 models, the canister is OK. If you get no reading, check the vacuum lines for restrictions. If you get higher readings, replace the canister.

Check idle speed

1 Connect a tachometer to the engine following the manufacturer's instructions. A typical hook-up connects one tachometer lead to the distributor (or negative) terminal on the coil and the other lead to a good ground.

2 Make sure any vacuum hoses not connected are plugged.

3 Start the engine and let it idle.

4 On both the Civic 1200 and the CVCC models, turn the idle-speed screw clockwise to increase the idle and counterclockwise to decrease it.

This typical idle-speed screw is found on Civic 1200's, 1977–79. The 1973–76 models have the screw on the left.

The CVCC carburetors used the same idle-speed screw from 1975–80. It is located on the right side of the carburetor near the firewall.

Set curb-idle speed

Set the curb-idle speed to the manufacturer's specifications for your particular model and year Honda. This information can be found on the underhood EPA sticker or in the owner's manual. The curb-idle speed is usually set with the engine warmed up and the choke valve fully opened. On 1973–79 Hondas, the lights should be turned on high beam. On 1980 models this is not necessary. Set Hondamatic transmissions in Drive and manual transmissions in Neutral. If the curb-idle speed is set in Drive, have a helper apply the brakes. You can also put a brick in front of each wheel and apply the emerency brake to hold the car while in Drive.

Set fast-idle speed

To set fast-idle, put the transmission in Park. On the Civic 1200 from 1973–79, simply pull the choke knob to the first detent position. Fast idle should read within specifications.

To set the fast-idle speed on CVCC manual

SCREWDRIVER

choke cars (1975–79 CVCC sedans and wagons and 1976–77 Accords), pull the choke knob to the second detent position. Fast idle should read within specifications after one minute.

If the fast-idle is too low on either the Civic 1200 or the manual-choke CVCC, carefully increase the dimension of the slot. If the fast-idle is too high, carefully reduce the dimension of the slot with a pair of needlenose pliers.

STOP 1978–79 Accords, 1979 Preludes, and all 1980 models have a more complex idle-speed adjustment which involves part of the emission control system. These models should be tested by a professional mechanic if a problem is suspected.

Factors affecting gas mileage

How do you compute your gas mileage? The only proper way is to do it after each fill-up. Divide the total number of gallons of gas (including tenths) it takes to fill the tank into the total number of miles driven since the last fill-up. As an example: Your car's odometer reads 15,525 miles at the beginning of the week. At the end of the week your fuel is low. You fill up again and the odometer reads 15,775 miles. So you drove 250 miles that week and let's say it took 8.5 gallons of fuel to fill the tank. Divide the 250 miles by the 8.5 gallons. Your car averaged 29.4 miles per gallon for that tankful. But this average doesn't mean typical gas mileage for your car. There are many variables in a given week's driving to take into account:

• Was that mileage figure calculated after you did a lot of stop-and-go or highway driving?
• At the pump, was your car pointing uphill or down? This will affect the amount of gas the tank will hold and thereby affect computed mileage.
• Winter-time driving will produce lower mileage than summer driving because of choke operation.
• Underinflated tires cause excessive rolling resistance so they will result in lower mileage figures than normal. Bias-ply tires, when compared to radials, offer more rolling resistance, as do snow tires, and this adversely affects mileage.
• Poor front alignment will reduce mileage.
• Improperly adjusted brakes (too tight) can cause low mileage figures.
• Naturally, a poorly tuned engine wastes gas.

Adjust idle mixture

Idle-mixture adjustments are critical to your car's specific exhaust emission levels as required by law. Also, idle-mixture adjustments are important to the economy of your car's performance. The following adjustment procedures should be considered general guidelines and temporary adjustments in the absence of the infra-red meter, exhaust-emission analyzer, and propane-assist (necessary for 1980 model Hondas) equipment used for the precise adjustment made by the professional mechanic. Since all Hondas originally came with limiter caps, the mixture adjustment should be done by a professional with sophisticated equipment. However, the method described here is OK for temporary adjustments when necessary.

To make this adjustment, you will need patience, a very small screwdriver (1980 models sold in California require a special Honda tool), and some dexterity because the mixture-adjusting screw is located in the back of the carburetor between it and the firewall on all Hondas from 1973–80. The engine must be at normal operating temperature, all vacuum lines not connected must be plugged, and the choke open.

IDLE-MIXTURE LIMITER CAP

1 Hook up a tachometer (see the chapter on Distributor Service).

2 Start the engine and allow it to idle.

3 Turn the headlamps on high beam (except on 1980 models) and put the Hondamatic-transmission models in Drive. Make sure the wheels are chocked and the emergency brake is engaged.

4 Remove the limiter cap.

5 Turn the idle-mixture screw clockwise until the rpm starts to drop significantly, even to the point of engine misfire.

6 Carefully observe the tachometer while turning the screw counterclockwise (not more than three turns) until the engine reaches its highest and/or smoothest idle.

7 Turn the idle-speed screw to about 50 rpm above the curb-idle speed indicated on the vehicle emission decal.

8 Slowly turn the idle-mixture screw clockwise until curb idle is again reached.

9 Reinstall the limiter cap.

10 If adjusting the idle-mixture screw does not improve engine performance, the carburetor should be rebuilt or replaced.

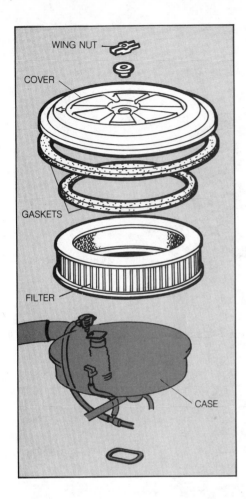

WING NUT

COVER

GASKETS

FILTER

CASE

Replace air-cleaner assembly

1 Set the bottom case of the air-cleaner assembly on the top of the carburetor.

2 Reattach all vacuum lines and hoses that were disconnected. Don't forget the electrical connection on models so equipped.

3 Make sure none of the hoses are pinched or kinked as you put the case in place.

4 Replace the attaching bolts and nuts.

5 Make sure the gaskets are in place.

6 Install the air filter in the air-cleaner assembly and fasten the cover with the wing nut and spring clips.

7 Double check that all hoses are attached, including the hot-air tube and fresh-air duct.

About vacuum leaks

SPREAD THIN LAYER OF OIL ON MATING SURFACES

An intake manifold vacuum leak will cause an engine to run and idle rough no matter how finely the carburetor is adjusted. If you suspect such a leak, here's how to detect it.

1 Place some light engine oil around the surface where the intake manifold contacts the cylinder head and where the carburetor contacts the intake manifold.

2 Start the engine. If the oil bubbles or the engine idle noticeably smoothes out, there is indeed a vacuum leak at one of the intake manifold or carburetor contact surfaces.

3 Re-torque the intake manifold and carburetor hold-down bolts to manufacturer's specifications. If the ret-torquing doesn't cure the problem, you'll have to replace the intake manifold or the carburetor gasket. To determine which gasket to replace, simply put the oil in the concentrated places until you find the leak.

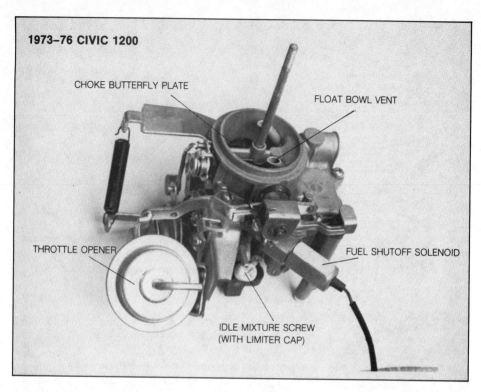

1973–76 CIVIC 1200

CHOKE BUTTERFLY PLATE

FLOAT BOWL VENT

THROTTLE OPENER

FUEL SHUTOFF SOLENOID

IDLE MIXTURE SCREW
(WITH LIMITER CAP)

1977–79 CIVIC 1200

CHOKE FAST-IDLE CAM

CHOKE BUTTERFLY BLADE

FUEL CUT-OFF SOLENOID

THROTTLE OPENER

IDLE MIXTURE SCREW
(WITH LIMITER CAP)

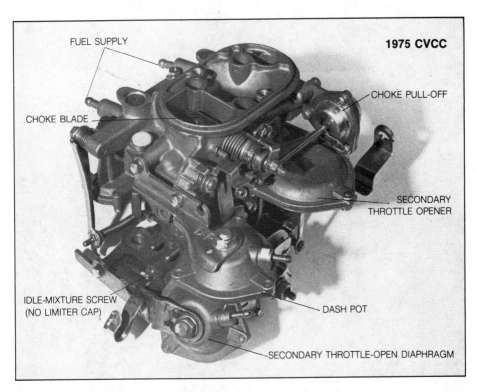

FUEL SUPPLY

1975 CVCC

CHOKE PULL-OFF

CHOKE BLADE

SECONDARY THROTTLE OPENER

IDLE-MIXTURE SCREW (NO LIMITER CAP)

DASH POT

SECONDARY THROTTLE-OPEN DIAPHRAGM

AIR VENT DIAPHRAGMS

CHOKE PULL-OFF

1978 CVCC ACCORD

CHOKE BLADE

SECONDARY THROTTLE OPENER

AUTO CHOKE COVER

FUEL CUT-OFF SOLENOIDS

FAST IDLE PULL-OFF

THROTTLE-OPEN DIAPHRAGM

IDLE-SPEED SCREW

IDLE-MIXTURE SCREW (LIMITER CAP)

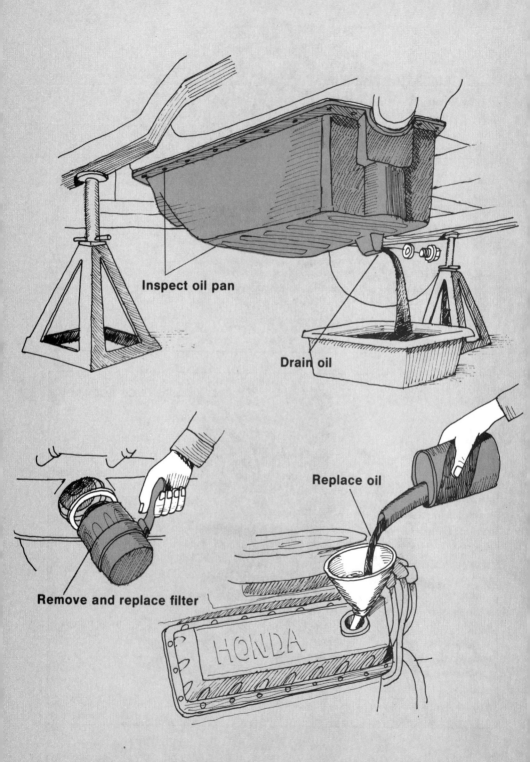

Inspect oil pan

Drain oil

Remove and replace filter

Replace oil

11

Oil System Service

PREP: Run the engine for about ten minutes to warm up the oil. Oil flows more easily when it's hot, so you will remove more dirt and contaminants when you drain the oil. Jack up the front of the car. For safety, support the front end on stands and chock the rear wheels.

1 Drain oil. Under normal driving conditions, follow the manufacturer's recommended maintenance schedule or change your engine oil every four to six months. For more severe driving conditions, cut this interval in half. On a Honda, make sure you are removing the oil pan drain plug, not the transmission plug, then be sure to replace the drain plug (p. 112).

2 Inspect oil pan. A pan that is punctured must be replaced. If the gasket has deteriorated to the point where it is leaking oil, it must be replaced (p. 112).

3 Remove and replace filter. It is best to replace the oil filter with every oil change because if you're going to the expense of putting in clean oil, why contaminate it immediately with the dirty oil left in the old filter? Make sure none of the old gasket remains on the block (p. 113).

4 Replace oil. Make sure you're using the correct type, grade, and amount. Doublecheck for any leaks (p. 114).

Essential. Basic tools • Jack • Wheel chocks • Safety stands • Drain pan • Cloths or paper towels • Oil filter wrench • Engine oil • Oil spout or funnel.
Handy. Fender cover.

Drain oil

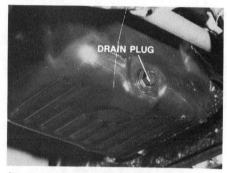

DRAIN PLUG

1 Warm the engine to operating temperature and raise the front of the car with safety stands.

2 Place a drain pan with a capacity of at least four quarts under the oil pan drain plug.

3 Loosen the drain plug and remove it and its washer by hand using a 17mm box-end wrench or sockets. *CAUTION: The oil is hot. To avoid burning your hands, remove the plug and washer carefully and quickly.*

🛑 Make sure you remove the oil pan drain plug, not the transmission plug.

4 Allow the oil to drain out completely into the drain pan. Since the Honda has a closed crankcase system, it facilitates draining if you remove the oil filler cap.

5 Clean the drain plug, especially the threads, with a cloth or paper towel.

6 Clean the washer. Since it is an aluminum crush washer, inspect it carefully for cracks. Replace if necessary.

7 Reinstall the washer and plug in the pan. If you have trouble replacing the plug, check the box in this chapter on repairing the drain plug.

🛑 Never use a wrench or socket to start the plug, and make sure you reinstall the washer.

Inspect oil pan

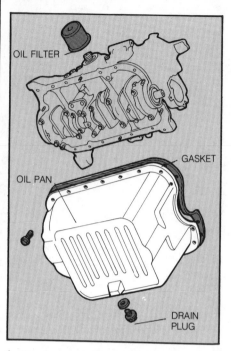

OIL FILTER

OIL PAN

GASKET

DRAIN PLUG

1 Check around the lip of the pan. If the gasket has deteriorated, there will be leakage and you should replace the gasket.

2 Look for leakage as a result of punctures or holes in the pan.

3 Replace the pan if you find such a condition.

4 Drain the oil.

5 Remove the pan bolts and take down the pan.

6 Replace the gasket, making sure none of the old gasket remains on the block.

To repair drain plug

Sometimes the threads in the oil pan drain hole are stripped because a faulty plug has been forced into the hole. If you have this problem, don't worry; you won't have to replace the oil pan. You can repair the drain hole with one of several drain plug repair kits on the market. One kit uses a self-tapping steel nut, which is forced into the pan's drain hole. A brass plug threads into the steel nut and becomes the new drain plug. Other kits use rubber stoppers, but they don't hold up as well as the steel nut.

To replace pan gasket

The Honda oil pan is sealed against the block with a neoprene gasket. The gasket is fitted to the oil pan with a small amount of silicone sealant in the area where the pan contacts the main bearing caps.

1 Remove the old silicone sealant.

2 Apply a small amount of new sealant to the same place as the old was applied. It is not necessary to apply the sealant to the entire gasket. If silicone sealant is not available, it is better to use none at all rather than gasket cement.

3 Torque the bolts evenly in a sequence from the center to both ends to avoid warping the pan.

To replace pan

1 Drain the oil.

2 Remove the bolts and take down the pan. When you replace the pan, make sure that the new one is the same size as the one you just removed and that the bolt holes line up.

3 Make sure the block face that the pan seals against is clean.

Remove and replace filter

1 Locate the filter. Although this can be done while you're under the car, you will probably have better access on some models from the engine compartment. The oil filter on all Hondas is located on the side of the engine close to the oil pan between the engine and the front of the car.

2 Put a drain pan in place below the filter.

3 Loosen the filter by turning it counterclockwise two turns using an appropriate oil filter wrench.

4 Remove the filter by hand when the oil has stopped draining into the pan.

🛑 There will still be some oil in the filter because of its angle, so remove it in an upright position to prevent spillage.

ECONOTIP Will switching to lower viscocity oil give better mileage? Yes, but the gain may be so small that you can't notice over short periods of time. The car has to be run through several tanks of gas to find out if it really helps your mileage. You must be careful, however, that you don't use too low a viscosity. Lighter oils don't have as much film strength, and that increases the chance of damaging the bearings, especially in an older car.

To change oil filter

When you go to buy a new oil filter, you should get the manufacturer's original equipment replacement filter. If you don't, make sure you buy a filter that has a built-in bypass system. To do so, you must know the year, make, and model of your car, and the cubic centimeter displacement (cc) of its engine. The cc displacement information can be found on the EPA emission sticker or in the owner's manual.

1 Clean the filter mating surface on the engine with a cloth and inspect the gasket and threads on the new filter.

2 Coat the filter gasket with a thin film of clean engine oil.

3 Thread the new filter onto the engine until the gasket lightly seats and then hand-tighten it three-fourths of a turn more. Tightening instructions are printed on the filter case or the box. Do not use an oil filter wrench.

Replace oil

1 Remove the oil filler cap located on the cylinder head cover.

2 Add the correct amount of oil to the crankcase using an oil spout or funnel. For most model Hondas, this amount is about 3.8 quarts with a filter change or about 3.2 quarts without a filter change. Check your owner's manual for your particular model and year. The oil should be a good 10W40 SE grade, but in extremely cold temperatures a 5W20 is acceptable as is a 20W50 in extremely hot climates.

3 Check the oil level and add more if necessary.

4 Start the engine and inspect for leaks around the filter and drain plug, then turn the engine off and let it set for a few minutes to allow the oil to drain back into the pan.

5 Remove the drain pan and properly dispose of the waste oil and filter.

6 Lower the car off the safety stands or ramps.

7 Recheck the oil level and add more if necessary.

To check oil level

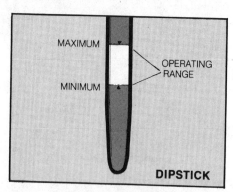

Engine oil should be kept at the MAX mark on the dipstick, although it is safe to wait until the level drops to the MIN mark before adding a quart. An engine should not be run if the oil level is one quart low, and the old wives' tales that the engine runs best that way are wrong. The oil should be checked when the car is on level ground and only after the engine has been shut off for at least a few minutes. This allows the oil in various parts of the engine to drain down to the crankcase.

1 Locate the dipstick. Normally it can be found protruding out of one side of the engine or the other. The dipstick is a long metal rod, one end of which is curled into a loop so it can be conveniently pulled out.

2 Remove the dipstick and wipe it clean with a cloth or paper towel. You should be able to see the markings MIN and MAX near the end of it.

3 Reinsert the dipstick into the tube, making sure to push it in as far as it will go.

4 Now pull it straight out, keeping it in a vertical position, and read the oil level. If the oil is at the MIN mark, you need a quart. If it is on the MAX mark, the level is OK. Once in a while when the car is very low on oil, you may not get a reading at all. In this case put in a quart of oil and take another reading. Continue to check the dipstick and add oil until the level is at MAX. Note: Do not overfill the engine with oil. This can cause the oil to foam when the engine is running and interfere with lubrication.

5 Doublecheck for any leaks.

To replace gasket on rocker arm valve cover

If, while pouring the oil into the oil filler hole, you noticed either oil coming from the cylinder head cover (valve cover) or an accumulation of old oil in the area of the valve cover where it mates with the cylinder head, you should replace the valve cover gasket.

1 Remove the air-cleaner assembly, the spark plug cable bracket, the throttle cable from its bracket, and the clutch cable and vacuum booster hose from their brackets, if applicable.

2 Unbolt the two 10mm retaining crown nuts and remove the bushings and washer from the valve cover. Then remove the cover.

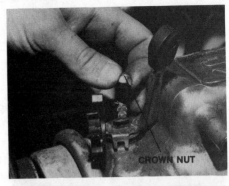

3 Visually inspect the camshaft, oil pump drive gear, rocker arms, and valve stems for wear and looseness.

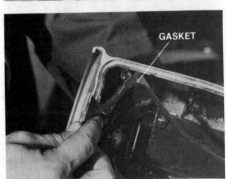

4 Remove the old neoprene gasket and replace it in its valve cover recess. Do not use gasket sealant.

5 Reinstall the valve cover with a new gasket, bushing, and washer. Then reinstall the cables and the air-cleaner assembly.

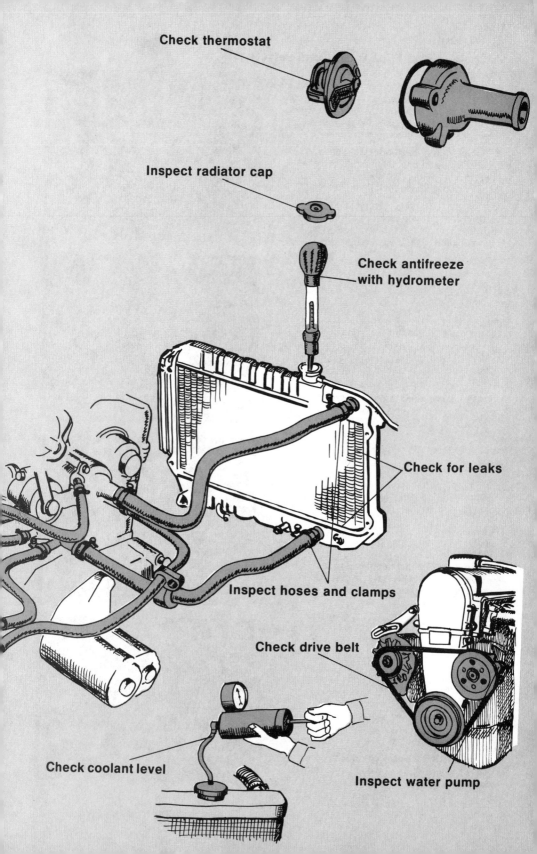

Check thermostat

Inspect radiator cap

Check antifreeze with hydrometer

Check for leaks

Inspect hoses and clamps

Check drive belt

Inspect water pump

Check coolant level

12

Cooling System Service

1 Check for leaks. Inspect the radiator around seams, petcocks, automatic transmission oil cooler connections, hose connections. Corrosion or antifreeze stains are a good indication there's a leak. Test for leaks with a pressure tester. Service the radiator and check the transmission oil (p, 118).

2 Inspect hoses and clamps. Check the rubber for cracks, softness, brittleness, leaks, swelling, and chafing. Replace any hoses with these conditions. Replace any broken or weak clamps (p. 121).

3 Inspect radiator cap. If it's loose, replace it. Check the pressure relief valve for firm spring action (p. 122).

4 Check coolant level. Coolant should at least cover the tubes inside the upper tank. Suspect a leak if the level is low. If there are signs of oil, rust or scales inside the filler neck, you may have an internal leak. Take a compression and/or pressure test. Clean and reverse-flush the system (p. 123).

5 Check antifreeze with hydrometer. For best production, maintain the system to conform to the coldest weather in your area (p. 124).

6 Inspect water pump. With the belt removed, grasp the pump pulley with both hands, turning and moving it inward and outward. If it makes a noise when you spin it, the bearings are worn. If you see signs of coolant leakage, the seals are probably damaged. Leaks and/or bad bearings mean the pump should be replaced (p. 125).

7 Check thermostat. Do this only if your engine is overheating. Replace a faulty thermostat and always replace the gasket. Never reuse the one you took off (p. 126).

8 Check drive belt. Turn the alternator pulley by hand. If it moves easily, the belt is slipping and should be adjusted. A belt that is too tight can cause more damage than a belt that is too loose (p. 127).

Essential. Basic tools • Antifreeze hydrometer • Pressure tester and cap adapter • Garden hose • Drain pan • Clean rags or towels • Putty knife or gasket scraper.
Handy. Flushing T • Filler neck deflector • Belt tensioner • Thermometer • Compression gauge • Torque wrench • Small socket set and universal • Wire brush or sandpaper.

Check for leaks

CAUTION: Your Honda utilizes a closed cooling system that is pressurized. In fact, with the proper mixture of antifreeze and a good pressure cap, the system's coolant temperature may exceed 250°F without boiling. Never remove the radiator cap when the system is hot.

The pressurized cooling system and coloring in the antifreeze make external leaks easy to locate visually. Inspect around the radiator seams, where the core is soldered to the upper and lower tanks, and around hose connections, petcocks, cylinder head gaskets, and, if your car has a Hondamatic transmission, at the connections of the transmission oil cooler lines. If there is an external leak, there may be telltale whitish corrosion or antifreeze stains. Leaks must be corrected mechanically. The radiator should be removed and taken to a specialist. If there are no visible signs of leakage, but your engine has been overheating or you have been replacing coolant frequently, perform a pressure leak test.

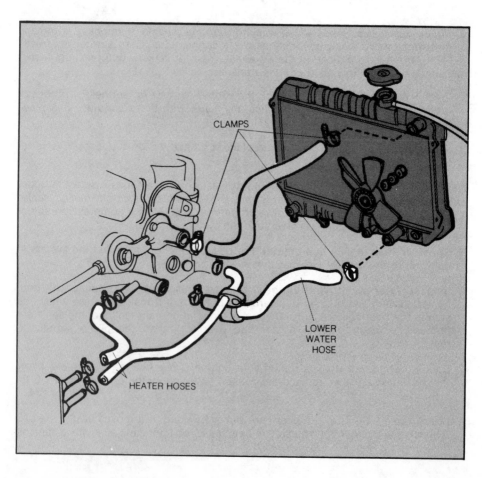

CLAMPS

LOWER
WATER
HOSE

HEATER HOSES

To test for leaks

1 With the engine cool, remove the radiator cap.

2 Start the engine and allow it to heat up to normal operating temperature. If necessary, add water to the cooling system because as the thermostat opens with the cap off, there will be some overflow of the coolant from the radiator.

3 Turn the engine off.

4 Install the pressure tester on the radiator filler neck, following the manufacturer's instructions.

5 Operate the pump of the radiator pressure tester until the gauge's needle reaches the pressure prescribed for your engine, between 11 and 14 psi for most Hondas. This forces coolant through the defective component. In some cases, a defective port may not show signs of a leak unless additional pressure is exerted into the cooling system.

STOP Never exceed the prescribed pressure in performing the pressure test. If you do, you may damage the cooling system by rupturing the radiator or splitting the hoses.

6 Look for leaks in the radiator hoses and connections, the heater itself, its hoses and connections, the thermostat housing gasket, the radiator tanks and core, and the water pump.

7 Take a gauge reading if no leaks are detected. The reading should hold for at least two minutes. If no leaks are detected visually, but the pressure gauge needle drops slowly, there may be an internal leak caused by a cracked block, cylinder head or water jacket. Have your car checked out by a professional mechanic in this case.

8 When the pressure test is completed, slowly release the pressure in the cooling system, following the manufacturer's instructions. On most models, you just push on the side of the hose near the cap part of the tester.

CAUTION: Release the pressure slowly and make sure all of it is released because you will test the coolant with the engine at normal operating temperature which is about 190°F. Use care, the engine is hot.

9 Remove the tester from the radiator, but leave the cap off to service the radiator.

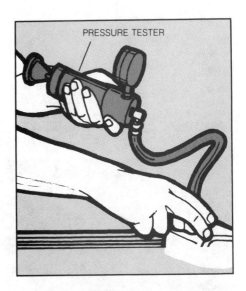

PRESSURE TESTER

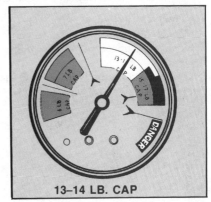

13–14 LB. CAP

PUSH HOSE TO RELEASE PRESSURE

To service the radiator

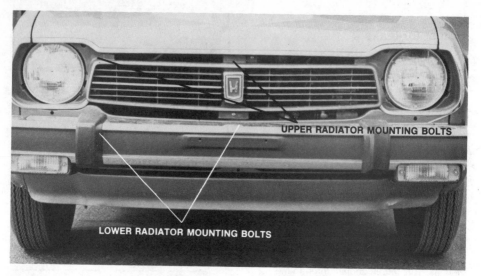

UPPER RADIATOR MOUNTING BOLTS

LOWER RADIATOR MOUNTING BOLTS

1 To remove the radiator, first drain the cooling system.

2 Remove the upper and lower radiator hoses.

3 Locate and disconnect the wires to the thermosensor in the bottom of the radiator. If your Honda is equipped with a Hondamatic transmission, you will have to loosen the connection at the radiator and disconnect the lines.

4 Remove the pan of coolant and place a clean pan under the cooler line connections to catch any transmission oil that may spill.

(STOP) Do not start the engine. If you do, you will lose all your transmission oil. And check the coolant for possible transmission fluid contamination.

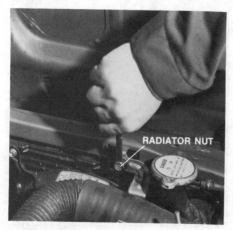

RADIATOR NUT

5 Locate the radiator supports and remove the support bolts. The four support bolts on the 1973–79 Civic, 1975–79 CVCC sedan and wagon, and 1976–80 Accord are accessible through the grille, but you will need a small socket set with a universal. And use care because the grille is plastic.

OR if you have a 1979–80 Prelude or a 1980 Civic or wagon, there are only two support bolts at the top of the radiator and they are accessible from the engine compartment.

(STOP) When servicing the radiator on any model Honda, it will be easier to remove the radiator, shroud, and cooling fan as one assembly and separate them after removal. When lifting the radiator assembly out, be careful not to rub it against any sharp objects that would damage it further.

6 Have the radiator repaired by a professional mechanic or buy a new one.

7 To install a repaired or new radiator, attach the fan and shroud. Carefully put the radiator in place and replace the support bolts.

8 Reconnect the transmission cooler lines, if your car is equipped with them.

9 Replace the thermosensor wires and the upper and lower radiator hoses.

10 Fill the cooling system with coolant.

11 Start the engine and allow it to reach normal operating temperature.

12 Replace the radiator cap and check for leaks.

To check the transmission oil

If your car is equipped with a Hondamatic transmission, you may have lost some of the transmission fluid when you disconnected the transmission oil cooler lines from the radiator. So when you button up the job, check the transmission fluid level and add oil if necessary.

To clean debris from the radiator

Use a garden hose to clean leaves, insects, and other debris from the radiator. Debris can restrict the flow of air through the radiator as well as retain heat, both of which may reduce the efficiency of the cooling system. For best results, apply water at high pressure from the engine side.

The radiator cooling system has many hoses—top and bottom hoses, two heater hoses, a by-pass hose, and on 1978–80 CVCC engines, there are two coolant hoses to the intake manifold. The average life of a radiator hose is about two years or 25,000 miles.

Inspect hoses and clamps

1 Check the hoses when the engine is cold. Look for cracks, softness, brittleness, leaks, swelling, and chafing. When you squeeze the hoses, they should feel firm, and when you release them, they should return to their original shape immediately. Pay particular attention to the bottom hose. Sometimes there is a spring inside it to prevent it from drawing closed. If this hose gets extremely rough treatment from the water pump, the spring can collapse if the hose softens. If the hose is loose or cracked, air can get into the system and cause rust. Soft hoses are particularly dangerous because they can deteriorate from the inside and small pieces of rubber may break off and clog the radiator and heater core.

2 Examine clamps and clamp areas, and replace any broken or weak clamps. Look for white or rust-colored deposits around the clamps. These indicate a leak. Try tightening the clamp to correct the leak. If this doesn't work, replace the clamp and/or the hose.

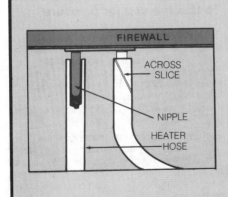

PRO SHOP After the heater, radiator, and by-pass hoses have been on a car for a long time, they tend to bond themselves to the connecting surfaces (nipples). This makes removal a real chore and can even damage the nipples if excessive force is used to remove the hoses. Make sure the engine is cool, then drain the coolant into a clean pan if you plan to reuse it. Removing a heater or by-pass hose is easier if you slice a diagonal cut into the hose near its end. The cut will relieve the tension on the hose fabric. Remember to refill the system with used or new coolant and recheck for leaks.

To replace hoses and clamps

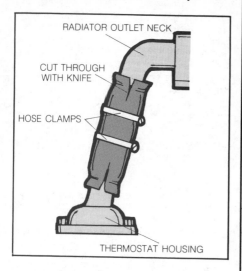

RADIATOR OUTLET NECK

CUT THROUGH WITH KNIFE

HOSE CLAMPS

THERMOSTAT HOUSING

Remove hoses when the engine is cool. If only the upper hose is to be replaced, open the petcock and drain out about two quarts of coolant. If the lower hose is to be replaced,

you must drain the radiator. If you want to reuse the coolant, drain it into a clean container.

1 Loosen the clamps and slide them away from the ends of the hose you are replacing, then twist the hose off the connections. If the hose is fused to the metal, slit it lengthwise and pry it off carefully with a screwdriver.

2 To install a new hose, first clean off the connectors, using either a wire brush or sandpaper. Slide the clamps onto the new hose and position them about one quarter of an inch from the ends. Twist the new hose onto the connectors, making sure the clamps are positioned past the raised beads. Tighten the clamps securely.

3 Close the petcock and refill the cooling system with the drained coolant or new coolant.

4 Start the engine and allow it to reach normal operating temperature, then check the coolant level. If necessary, add antifreeze.

5 Replace the radiator pressure cap.

6 Allow the engine to run long enough to build up pressure in the system, at least four or five minutes, then check all hose connections for leaks.

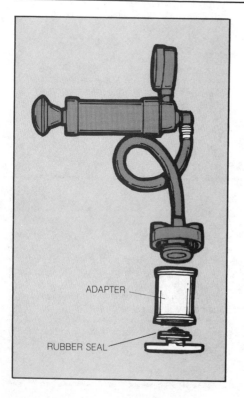

ADAPTER

RUBBER SEAL

Inspect radiator cap

Pressure caps are important to the cooling system. They increase the temperature at which coolant boils, increase water pump efficiency, and eliminate coolant loss due to evaporation. Defective caps can cause over-heating, which could ultimately result in engine damage. A radiator cap should fit tightly on the filler neck. Replace it if it's loose. Inspect the pressure relief valve. Its spring action should be firm when you press down on it.

To test the cap for pressure

1 Connect a radiator pressure cap adapter, supplied with a pressure tester, to make a more accurate check of relief pressure. Wet the cap's rubber seal with water and connect it to the adapter. Read the markings on the pressure cap to determine the rated capacity in pounds per square inch (psi), 11 to 14 on most Hondas.

2 Pump the pressure tester until the gauge reads the rated capacity of the cap. This pressure reading should hold for at least two minutes. If the pressure drops before that time, the radiator cap is defective and should be replaced.

Check coolant level

The coolant should be within one inch of the bottom of the fill neck and up to the full mark in the coolant reservoir with the engine at normal operating temperature. If you have been replacing coolant frequently, or if signs of oil, rust or scales are found inside the upper tank, you may have a leak. While you may not be able to correct this kind of problem, you can take a compression test and/or pressure test to confirm if and what kind of leak may exist. If the test proves negative, clean and reverse-flush the system. If the test proves positive, have a professional mechanic check out your cooling system.

To reverse-flush the radiator

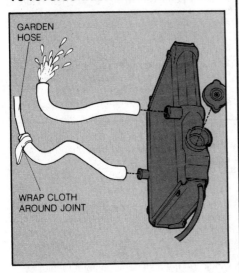

GARDEN HOSE

WRAP CLOTH AROUND JOINT

Reverse-flush the radiator every two years with your antifreeze change.

1 Drain the cooling system by removing the radiator cap, opening the petcock, and disconnecting the lower hose.

2 Disconnect the upper radiator hose from the thermostat housing and the lower hose from the water pump inlet tube.

3 Close the petcock and replace the pressure cap.

4 Position the opening of the upper hose so it's pointing toward the ground, away from the engine.

5 Insert a garden hose into the lower radiator hose opening and wrap a piece of cloth around the joint to seal it.

6 Turn on the garden hose and allow water to flow into the lower section of the radiator, up through the radiator, and out through the upper radiator hose. Keep the water flowing until it is clear.

7 Reconnect the hoses if for some reason you are not reverse-flushing the block.

To reverse-flush the block

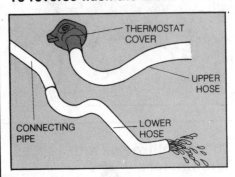

THERMOSTAT COVER

UPPER HOSE

CONNECTING PIPE

LOWER HOSE

Reverse-flush the block when you change the antifreeze and anytime you reverse-flush the radiator.

1 Remove the thermostat and replace the thermostat housing gasket or the O-ring on models so equipped. Now's a good time to check the thermostat (see the instructions later on in this chapter).

2 Disconnect the upper radiator hose at the radiator, but leave it connected to the thermostat housing.

3 Disconnect the lower radiator hose at the radiator, but leave it connected to the water pump inlet tube.

4 Position the hose so the opening faces the ground, away from the engine.

5 Insert a garden hose in the opening of the upper hose.

6 Allow the water to flow through the engine block and out of the water pump through the lower hose to the ground until the water runs clear.

7 Replace the thermostat, housing, and gasket or O-ring, and reconnect the upper and lower hoses. Add the proper amount of antifreeze, then fill the radiator with fresh water. Start the engine and allow it to reach normal operating temperature. Now check the coolant level, top off with fresh water if necessary, reinstall the pressure cap, and check for leaks.

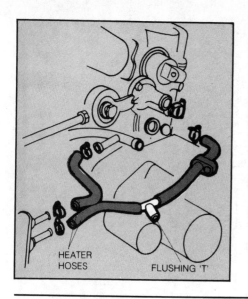

HEATER HOSES   FLUSHING 'T'

To use a flushing T

You can reverse-flush both the radiator and the block by hooking up a flushing T. The advantage of the T is that, once connected, it can be left on the car and used year after year, thus avoiding all the hose disconnecting and reconnecting involved in the two previous steps.

1 Attach a flushing T to the heater-supply hose. That's the hose that comes from the engine. Don't mistake it for the hose that runs to the water pump. The T should be situated so water pouring from it does not get on the starter. If your radiator has an exceptional amount of grease buildup or corrosion, you may want to use a one-step, fast-flushing agent.

2 Replace the antifreeze after reverse-flushing the cooling system. Remember to remove the cap from the T when adding the antifreeze until it flows out the T.

Check antifreeze with hydrometer

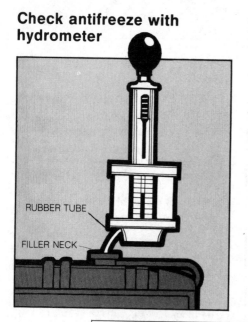

RUBBER TUBE

FILLER NECK

1 Remove the radiator cap when the engine is cold.

2 Start the engine and allow it to reach normal operating temperature.

3 Hold the hydrometer at eye level and read the scale. Some hydrometers use floating balls to indicate the freezing point, while others use a floating degree scale. For best antifreeze protection, the cooling system should be maintained to conform to the coldest weather in your area. If additional antifreeze is necessary to maintain the desired degree of protection, add enough to reach a 60/40 mixture of antifreeze to water. Anything less will reduce heat transfer and corrosion protection properties. To add antifreeze, you first may have to drain some coolant from the radiator.

STOP Remember your Honda has an aluminum head and many have an aluminum block. This means you should never use straight water without antifreeze or methanol or alcohol base antifreeze alone.

ETHYLENE GLYCOL-TYPE COOLANT MIXTURE					
* Cooling system capacity	Quarts of anti-freeze will protect to these temperatures				
	1 qt.	2 qts.	3 qts.	3½ qts.	4 qts.
4 qts.	10°F	−34°F	−68°F	−36°F	
5 qts.	13°F	−18°F	−57°F	−68°F	−57°F

*Average Honda cooling system capacity is 4.3 qts.

Inspect water pump

Most water pumps are lubricated and sealed at the factory and normally do not require maintenance. But bearings, seals, and the impeller blades do wear out. The most common cause of bearing failure is excessive tightening of the alternator belt.

1 Remove the alternator belt and grasp the pulley in both hands. Turn and move it inward and outward. If there's a rough,

grinding or loose feeling, the bearings are probably worn.

2 Check the ventilation hole below and behind the pulley by running your hand over it. If the seal is leaking, your hand will get wet from the coolant. Sand, rust, and other abrasive materials in the coolant will wear away the impeller blades. Corrosion of the impeller blades and housing may also result from using an antifreeze with inadequate corrosion and rust inhibitors.

3 Replace a water pump that has a leak or worn bearings.

To replace the water pump

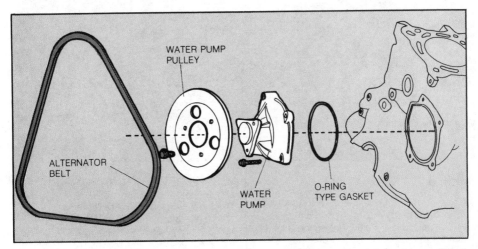

On the Civic 1200 models from 1973–79, the water pump is on the left as you look straight across the engine compartment from the driver's side of the car. The pump is on the right side of the engine on all CVCC models from 1975–80. The following replacement procedures apply to both models.

To remove the water pump

1 Drain the system.

2 Remove the three bolts holding the water pump pulley to the pump before loosening the alternator belt. If the pulley turns while removing the bolts, apply pressure on the alternator belt to help hold the pulley stationary.

3 Loosen the alternator and remove the belt.

4 Remove the four water pump bolts, the timing cover bracket, and the old pump.

5 Make sure the new pump is identical to the old one.

6 Install a new O-ring type gasket on the new pump. The pump can only be properly installed one way, with the vent hole at the bottom.

7 Reinsert each mounting bolt in its proper hole. Remember there are two different length bolts used to install the pump.

8 Clean the mating surface of the engine block and water pump thoroughly with a clean cloth to insure a good seal.

To reinstall the water pump

1 Position the pump against the engine and start all the bolts by hand only. Don't forget the timing cover bracket.

2 Push the pump in toward the engine until it is properly seated against the block and tighten the bolts evenly, then torque to about eight foot-pounds. Don't overtighten.

3 Replace the water pump pulley and tighten the bolts. They may be more easily tightened with the alternator belt installed and properly tensioned.

4 Replace the coolant and warm up the engine to normal operating temperature.

5 Bring the coolant up to the proper level and install the pressure cap.

6 Run the engine for a few more minutes and then check for leaks.

Check thermostat

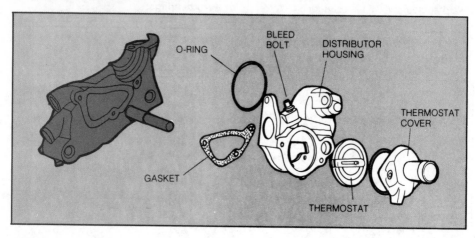

O-RING · BLEED BOLT · DISTRIBUTOR HOUSING · THERMOSTAT COVER · GASKET · THERMOSTAT

Method 1

An easy way to check your thermostat is to remove the radiator cap and insert a thermometer into the radiator. After starting the engine, watch the thermometer. The temperature on the thermometer should again begin to climb and the thermostat should start opening when the coolant begins to flow. Check this by squeezing the upper radiator hose. You will be able to feel the coolant flowing as the engine warms.

Method 2

1 Remove the thermostat and put it and a thermometer (which reads up to at least 250°) into a pan of water. This method is more complicated but more accurate than Method 1.

2 Heat the water and note when the thermostat starts to open. Continue to watch it until it is fully open.

3 To check the opening temperature, attach a .003-inch feeler gauge to a wire or string and position the gauge between the valve and the housing. When the gauge can be pulled free, you know the thermostat has

started to open. Most Honda thermostats should start to open around 180°F. Thermostats are designed to start to open at this temperature and should be fully opened about 20 degrees higher (about 200°F). If the thermostat doesn't meet specs, you should replace it.

To replace the thermostat

1 Drain the radiator and disconnect the upper radiator hose from the thermostat housing.

2 Remove the two bolts holding the housing to the cylinder head, but do not remove the third bolt close to the housing, since this would require replacing an extra gasket and O-ring and retiming the distributor.

3 Scrape the old gasket from the housing with a putty knife, if necessary on your model Honda. Don't use a screwdriver. Most CVCC models use an O-ring instead of a gasket.

4 Lift the thermostat out after noting how it was installed.

5 Install the new thermostat, with the

spring part around the temperature sensor, into the distributor housing.

6 Reinstall the housing and bolts.

7 Check the thermostat for correct alignment and make sure it doesn't slip down. Also be sure to install a new gasket or O-ring, depending on which was removed, but do not use gasket cement.

8 Torque the thermostat mounting bolts to about nine foot-pounds. Don't overtighten.

9 Refill the radiator, making sure you have an adequate amount of antifreeze regardless of the season. A 60/40 mixture of antifreeze and water is best for year-round protection.

10 Start the engine and run it until it reaches normal operating temperature, then reinstall the radiator cap and check for leaks.

Check drive belt

A loose, worn or missing alternator belt can cause as serious an overheating problem as a bad water pump. Inspect the undersides of all belts by twisting them. If they are cracked, cut, frayed, glazed or covered with grease, you should replace them. Turn the alternator pulley by hand. If it moves easily, the belt is slipping and should be adjusted. More damage can be caused by a belt which is too tight than by one which is too loose.

How to bleed the cooling system

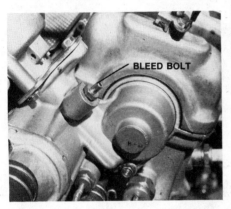

BLEED BOLT

The Honda has a cooling-system bleed bolt, which releases trapped air from the system. The bolt on the Civic 1200 is located on the

intake manifold next to the thermostat housing. On CVCC models, the bolt is on the distributor housing. Use the bleed bolt any time you refill the cooling system, notably after such jobs as radiator repair or replacement, hose and clamp repair or replacement, cooling system flushing, water pump replacement, thermostat and gasket replacement or coolant replacement.

1 Loosen the bleed bolt by turning it counterclockwise.

2 Fill the radiator. As the cooling system fills and the trapped air escapes, coolant will start flowing.

3 Close the bleed port at this point and finish filling the radiator and coolant reservoir.

4 Start the engine and run it until it reaches normal operating temperature.

5 Replace the radiator cap and check for leaks.

ECONOTIP Air conditioners put extra loads on engines and reduce mileage. They have the greatest effect on mileage in stop-and-go, hot weather driving. This, of course, is when you need the air conditioner the most. But if you can leave it off and suffer through the heat, you may avoid the average mileage reduction of nine percent which results from having the air conditioner on.

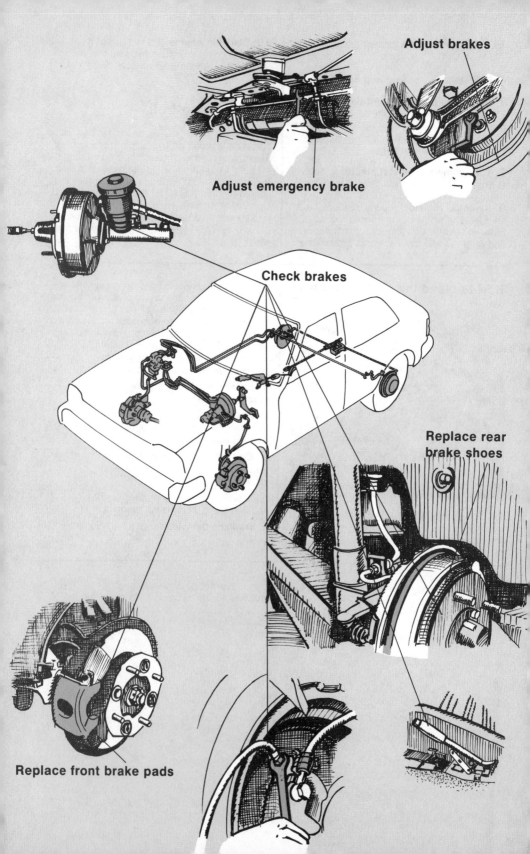

Adjust brakes

Adjust emergency brake

Check brakes

Replace rear brake shoes

Replace front brake pads

13

Brake System Service

1 Check brakes. Look at the front wheels. If there is an excessive amount of black dust on a wheel not too long after the last inspection, have it checked by a professional mechanic. Check the brake fluid. If it's low, check for leaks. Remove the wheels. Inspect the front rotors and pads. Remove the rear drums. Inspect the bearings, drums, and brake shoes. If there is less than $1/16$-inch on the pads or shoes, they should be replaced (p. 130).

2 Replace front brake pads. After removing the wheels, inspect the front rotors. If they're scored or excesssively worn or warped, you must have them replaced by a professional mechanic. However, if just the pads are worn, you may replace them yourself. Inspect the inside of the rotor and of the shoe very carefully (p. 133).

3 Replace rear brake shoes. Remove the tire-and-wheel assembly. Inspect for scores, ridges, heat spots, and check outs of round for excessive wear. Inspect the brake shoes. If there is less than $5/64$-inch, they must be replaced. Inspect the wheel cylinder, if leaking it must be replaced (p. 143).

4 Adjust brakes. If brake inspection reveals that the brakes are OK, they only need adjusting. With the emergency brake released, adjust the rear brakes by turning the adjuster bolt (p. 146).

5 Adjust emergency brake. The rear brakes must be adjusted before adjusting the emergency brake. The emergency brake is adjusted by using the adjusting nut (p. 147).

Essential. Basic tools • Special brake adjusting tool or long 7mm open-end wrench • Jack • Safety stands • Torque wrench • Wire brush • Sandpaper.
Handy. Fender cover • Droplight or flashlight • Brake measuring tool • C-clamp.

Check brakes

CAUTION: Limit your brake system repair and replacement jobs to those described in this chapter. Parts of the brake system are very complex and repairs must be made only by a professional mechanic. Remember, your car's brakes are its primary safety system. The brakes must be kept in good working order, and there are many jobs you can do yourself. But before you begin any job, make sure you understand every step.

To inspect front wheels

Most front disc-brake cars will develop a small amount of black dust (disc pad dust) over a period of time. However, a large amount in a short period of time usually means the front discs have too much drag. Either the brakes are constantly engaged even though the pedal is not touched or you're riding with your foot on the brake pedal. If your driving habits are not at fault, you should have the condition checked by a professional mechanic because the problem could be the hydraulic system, especially if it occurs only on one side.

To inspect brake pedal play

If your brake pedal is lower than normal or if it feels spongy, this could be an indication of an impending brake problem. A slight decrease in brake pedal height will occur as the brakes become worn and out of adjustment. This at least indicates the brakes need adjusting. If the pedal feels spongy rather than firm, it usually means that there is either air in the hydraulic system or a fluid leak. Also check for unusually long play in the pedal before the brakes begin to take hold, especially if the pedal sinks all the way to the floor.

To check emergency brake

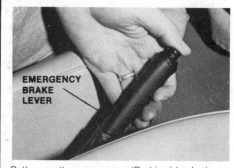

EMERGENCY BRAKE LEVER

Pull up on the emergency (Parking) brake lever and you should be able to stop the car. Raising the lever only three to seven clicks should keep it from moving. If it takes more than seven clicks of the lever, inspect the rear brakes for wear and adjust them before adjusting the emergency brake. Note: Some squealing and squeaking of the disc brake is normal, if it occurs after the brake pedal has been applied and just before the car stops rolling. If a rubbing, scraping or metal-against-metal sound is heard, check it or have it checked immediately.

To inspect fluid level

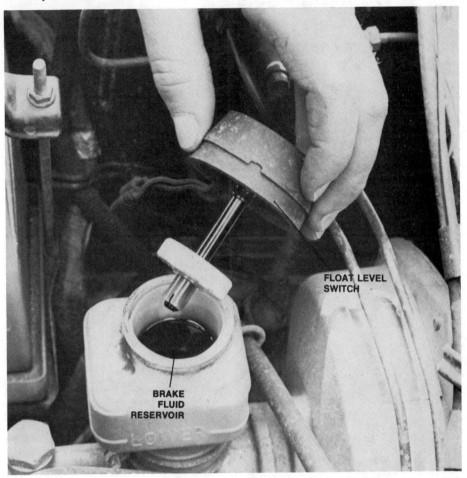

FLOAT LEVEL
SWITCH

BRAKE
FLUID
RESERVOIR

Every time you change the engine oil, check the level of the brake fluid in the master cylinder reservoir (1973–76 Hondas have two reservoirs; 1977–80 models have only one).

1 Locate the master cylinder under the hood, which on many models is on the passenger side, remove the top(s), and look at the level. As the fluid gets darker, you will be able to see the level through the plastic reservoir(s). The level should be up to the MAX line or about ½-inch from the top. Brake fluid absorbs moisture readily and also deteriorates chemically over time, so it should be replaced completely every couple of years.

2 If you add to or replace the fluid, make sure the label on the can says "meets DOT-3 or -4 specifications." Don't buy more than a pint at a time, replace the lid on the can very tightly, and since it is poisonous, store it carefully. Discard any unused fluid left in the can after a year.

3 Put the top(s) back on the master cylinder reservoir(s). If any dirt gets in, you will have to drain and replace all the fluid in the system.
Note: On cars equipped with disc brakes, a slightly lower-than-normal fluid level does not necessarily mean there is a leak in the system. As disc brake linings wear, the piston moves outward to compensate for it, and brake fluid takes up the displaced area behind the piston. For this reason, disc brakes require a greater amount of fluid. However, even with disc brakes, a low level is a warning there may be a leak in the system, so always check.

To check for leaks and cracks

Remove the front wheels one by one and check the following:

1 Check the caliper assembly for fluid leakage or a cracked casing.

2 Inspect the linings and pads and all hydraulic brake lines. Look for leaks, cracks, lines that have become thin by rubbing against a suspension part, and any other signs of wear or deterioration. *CAUTION: Do not attempt to disconnect any hydraulic lines yourself. Also, don't try to replace the master cylinder, a wheel cylinder or a caliper assembly. These tasks should be left to a professional mechanic.*

3 Carefully inspect the master cylinder and reservoir(s) and interconnecting lines for leaks, cracks or damage. If you notice a residue of brake fluid around a connection or fitting, try to torque it. If this doesn't help, have a professional mechanic repair it.

Replace front brake pads

The disc brake system uses a heavy disc instead of a drum, and brake friction pads rather than brake shoes and linings. In place of the wheel cylinder, a caliper is bolted to the wheel spindle so the friction pads on the caliper can sandwich the disc between them. When pressure is exerted on the brake pedal, the fluid in the caliper moves the pistons, which in turn forces the friction pads against the disc, stopping the car. Honda uses four different disc brake caliper assemblies on the front, depending on the model. Locate the instructions for your model and follow them carefully.

Civic

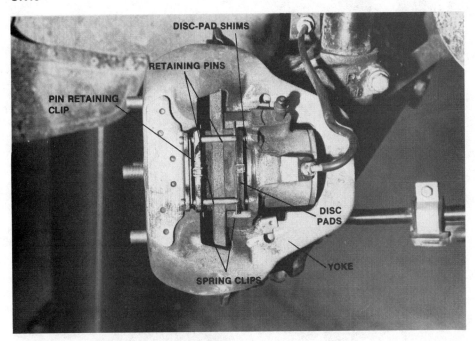

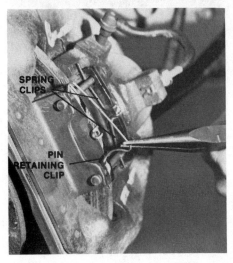

This disc brake caliper assembly is found on 1973–79 Civic 1200 models, 1975–79 CVCC sedans, and 1975 wagons. With the car jacked up and on safety stands, remove the tire-and-wheel assembly.

1 Pull the pin retaining clip out of the pad retaining pins with a pair of needlenose pliers.

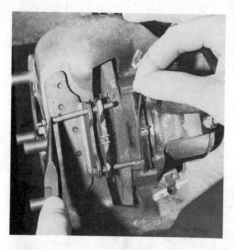

2 Remove the upper pad retaining pin, then the other pin, carefully noting the location of the pad spring clips. This is necessary because as you pull the pin, the clips are spring-loaded and will become airborne.

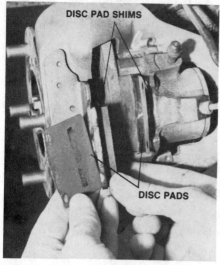

DISC PAD SHIMS

DISC PADS

3 Remove the pads and brake pad shims. Most of the newer models have a teflon-coated pad next to the pad instead of shims.

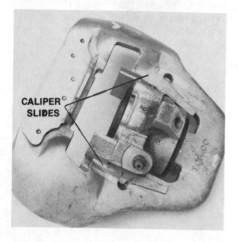

CALIPER SLIDES

4 To move the pistons into the caliper use an old pad held against the piston. Make sure the caliper slides are free of dirt and corrosion. If not, clean and lubricate the slide area with a good high-temperature lubricant.

PIN

5 Clean the retaining pins of any dirt, rust or corrosion with a wire brush. If they're badly pitted, replace them.

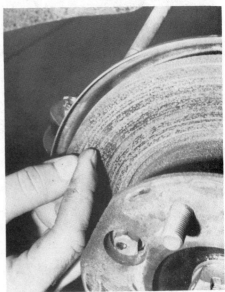

6 Carefully inspect the rotor for cracks or deep grooves. If the rotor is badly scarred or cracked, it must be replaced by a professional mechanic because the hub and rotor are press-fitted into the front axle bearings and require special equipment for removal. Be sure not to get any grease, brake fluid or lubricant on the disc pads or the rotor surface. If you do, wipe it off with alcohol.

7 Insert the new brake pads (be sure they are facing toward the rotors) and brake pad shims between the caliper piston and the rotor on one side and between the rotor and yoke. The arrangement from the outside in should be: Yoke, brake pad shims (if they are the coated type, put them against the pad back), new brake pad, rotor, new brake pad, brake pad shims (coated side against the pad back), caliper piston. To complete reassembly, reverse the above procedure and install a pad retaining pin and spring clips. Slide the other pad retaining pin under the other end of the spring clips and then install the pin retaining clip.

8 Repeat the above procedure on the other front wheel, then complete the final check.

9 Fill the master cylinder reservoir(s) with high-temperature brake fluid (only DOT 3 or 4) and replace the reservoir cover(s).

10 Pump the brake pedal several times until it is firm and the pads have been properly seated and the caliper filled.

11 Recheck the brake fluid level in the master cylinder, inspect for leaks, and reinstall the tire-and-wheel assemblies, torquing to 65 foot pounds.

Wagon

The front of the 1976–80 wagon has a different front-brake caliper assembly from the Civic. If your inspection of the front brake assembly reveals that only the brake pads are worn below a safe limit, you can replace the pads yourself. They may be replaced without removing or disassembling the brake caliper. Place the car on safety stands and remove the wheel assembly.

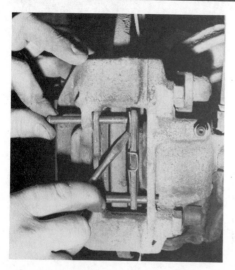

PRO SHOP It may be easier to gradually start one retaining pin. Put the outer shim (with coated side towards the disc-pad backing plate) onto the outer pad, then the rotor. Work the retaining pin through the inner pad, the shim, and into the caliper. Now install the other retaining pin and retaining clips and the pad shield.

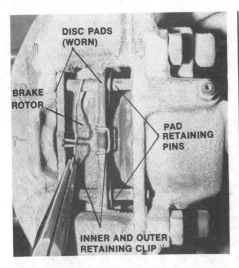

DISC PADS (WORN)

BRAKE ROTOR

PAD RETAINING PINS

INNER AND OUTER RETAINING CLIP

1 **Remove the outer retaining clip** from the hole in the outer disc pad. Slide that clip down through the hole in the lower retaining pin until the clip comes out of the upper retaining pin.

2 **Unhook the other (inner) retaining clip** from over the inner disc pad, then slide this clip into one of the retainer pins until it can be lifted out. The two retaining pins are now ready for removal.

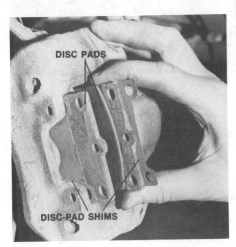

DISC PADS

DISC-PAD SHIMS

3 **Pull the pins out** and then lift the disc pads and shims straight up. No further disassembly is required to replace the pads.

STOP Be sure no one steps on the brake pedal during this procedure, since this may make the piston in the caliper pop out, causing a hydraulic leak.

4 **Use a C-clamp or two screwdrivers and the old disc pad to push on the caliper piston** until it is recessed into the caliper bore. Apply equal pressure on the piston so you don't cock it in its bore.

5 **Clean any dirt and rust from the caliper and retaining pins,** using only a wire brush and a hand cloth. Then inspect the caliper for fluid leaks. If fluid is leaking from the caliper piston, reassemble the old disc pads and the caliper, and take the car to a mechanic for repair.

6 **Visually inspect the rotors** for cracks, scoring, wear or deep grooves. If the rotors are abnormally worn, take the car to a professional mechanic because the rotor (disc) and hub are pressed into the axle bearings and this work requires special equipment.

7 **Insert the new disc pads into the caliper** by reversing the disassembly procedure. Make sure the friction material (not the metal side) is facing the rotors. Also be sure the pads are well seated into the caliper and the retaining pin is inserted.

8 **Repeat this procedure on the other wheel,** then complete the final step. Fill the master cylinder reservoir(s) with DOT 3 or 4 brake fluid, replace the cover(s) on the master cylinder reservoir(s), and pump the brake pedal several times to fill the caliper. Check for leaks and replace the tire-and-wheel assembly to the wheel lug nuts with 65 foot-pounds of torque.
CAUTION: After completing any brake work, begin your road test cautiously, at low speed. Don't thoroughly road test your car until you have made sure you have full braking power.

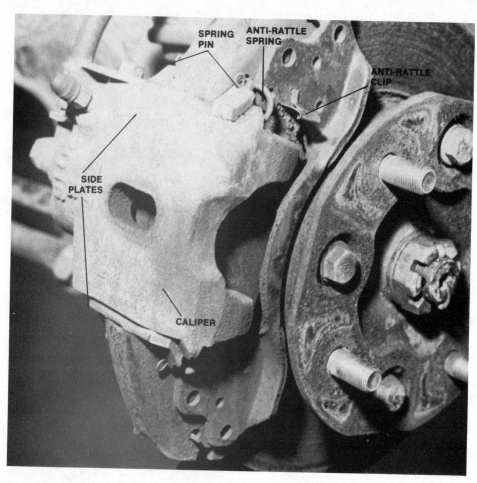

SPRING
PIN

ANTI-RATTLE
SPRING

ANTI-RATTLE
CLIP

SIDE
PLATES

CALIPER

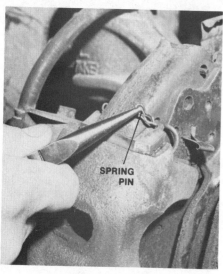

SPRING
PIN

Accord

A third type of front disc brake caliper assembly is found on the 1976–80 Accords, including the LX and 4-door models.

1 Put the car up on safety stands and remove the wheel assembly, then remove the four spring pins from the slide plates using a pair of pliers. Note the position of the spring pins in the holes of the slide plate for easier reassembly. The entire spring pin is in the hole, not between the edge and the hole of the slide.

2 Remove the side plates by sliding them toward you. Once the first one is removed, the second slide plate will just about fall out. If the slide plates do not slide out, carefully use a drift pin and hammer to coax them out. With the slide plates removed, the caliper body and piston can be lifted out of the anchor plate at an angle to expose the rotor sandwiched between the disc brake pads.

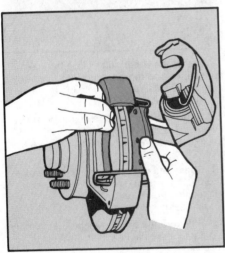

3 Now remove both disc brake pads by pulling them straight out to the sides. Note the location of the anti-rattle clips on the upper end of each pad. Also note that under the inner pad there is another anti-rattle clip (this one is elongated and only under one pad, not both). Do not confuse these anti-rattle clips with the two anti-rattle springs which do not have to be removed for disc pad replacement.

PRO SHOP You can effectively support the caliper by looping one end of a wire coat hanger around one of the coils of the Mac-Pherson strut and the other end around the caliper body.

ECONOTIP There are many city streets that are uncongested enough to invite higher than normal speeds. But often these streets have timed traffic lights every few blocks. Just about the time your car gets up to a good cruising speed, you get caught by the next light. By looking ahead and lowering your speed to reach the light just after it turns green, you will save a lot of gas and arrive at your destination as fast as the driver who speeds up and has to stop for every light.

4 **Using one of the old brake pads and a C-clamp, compress the piston** back into the caliper body.

5 **Clean and inspect the calipers, rotors, and slide plates.** Clean excess dirt and rust from the caliper and inspect them for cracks and leaks. Inspect the rotors for cracks, scoring, grooves, and excessive rust. If any of these conditions exist and the rotor(s) need replacing, you must have it done by a professional mechanic because the hub and rotor are press-fitted into the front axle bearings and special equipment is necessary.

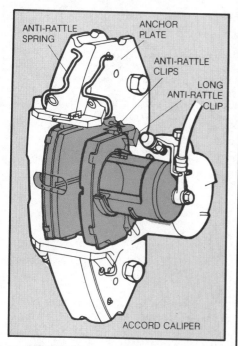

ANTI-RATTLE SPRING

ANCHOR PLATE

ANTI-RATTLE CLIPS

LONG ANTI-RATTLE CLIP

ACCORD CALIPER

6 **To install new front disc pads, simply reverse the disassembly procedure.** First install the long anti-rattle clip located under the inner disc pad. Then fasten the other two anti-rattle clips to the anchor plate on the upper end.

7 **Slide the two disc pads in** with the teflon-coated brake pad shim against the backing plate of the disc pad.

8 **Install the caliper body** over the pads, shims, and rotor.

9 **With the caliper in place and the anti-rattle spring under the ledge of the caliper, hold the caliper up** and slide the slide plate into place.

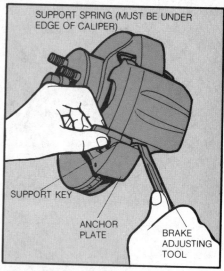

SUPPORT SPRING (MUST BE UNDER EDGE OF CALIPER)

SUPPORT KEY

ANCHOR PLATE

BRAKE ADJUSTING TOOL

10 **Insert the other slide plate between the caliper and the anchor plate.** Then install the four spring pins into the holes of the slide plates.

11 **Repeat the procedure** on the other front wheel and then pump the brake pedal several times until it is firm and the pads are seated.

12 **Check the master cylinder reservoir and fill,** if necessary, with only high-temperature brake fluid (DOT 3 or 4) and check for signs of leakage.

13 **Reinstall the tire- and wheel-assembly** and torque the wheel lug nuts to 65 foot-pounds.

Breaking in pads

Drive with extra care for the first 1000 miles after replacing your brake pads. Avoid sudden stops, harsh braking or high speed driving that would overheat the rotors. Until the pads are properly seated, a careless driver can easily damage the pads and rotors.

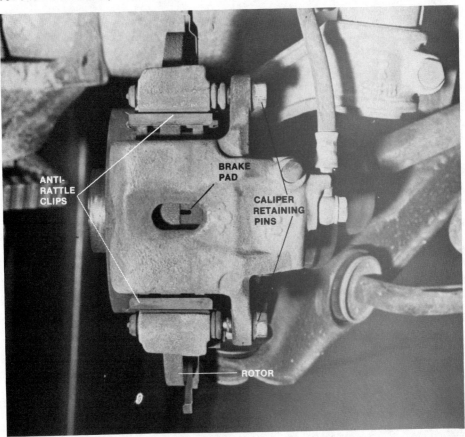

ANTI-RATTLE CLIPS

BRAKE PAD

CALIPER RETAINING PINS

ROTOR

The newest and probably the easiest front disc brake assembly to work on is found on 1979 and 1980 Preludes and 1980 Civics.

1 Secure the car for your safety and place the front of the car on safety stands. Chock the rear wheels and remove the front tire-and-wheel assembly.

2 Loosen the upper caliper retaining pin about two turns with the wheel turned out. Then remove the lower caliper retaining pin (do not confuse the caliper retaining pins with the caliper mounting bolts).

3 With the upper retaining pin loosened and the lower pin removed, swing the caliper body up, pivoting it on the upper pin. Do this carefully to avoid bending the anti-rattle clips. Take a close look at the clips' location. Although it is easy to work on, it is difficult to explain how to seat the anti-rattle clips properly.

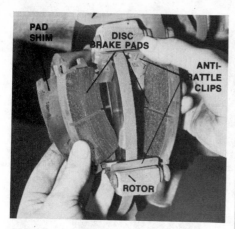

PAD SHIM · **DISC BRAKE PADS** · **ANTI-RATTLE CLIPS** · **ROTOR**

4 Remove the brake pad shim and brake pads by sliding them out of the anti-rattle clips and caliper mount.

5 Clean the caliper mount and body and inspect for damage or cracks, being careful not to disturb the caliper piston. Also inspect the rotor carefully for cracks, grooves, and scoring. If you find any of these conditions, the rotor must be replaced. Unlike the other model Hondas, the Prelude and 1980 Civic rotors can be replaced by the average do-it-yourselfer.

BOLTS AS PULLER · **RETAINING SCREW BEING REMOVED**

6 If the rotor on a 1979 or 1980 Prelude or a 1980 Civic has to be replaced and if the wheel bearings are OK, you can do the job yourself. Remove the two caliper mounting bolts, lift the caliper, and hold it out of the way with a coat hanger or mechanic's wire. On Prelude models, remove the small disc retaining screw (this is not found on the 1980 Civics). Note: This is a Prelude which accepts lug bolts (the 1980 Civic uses lug nuts). As rust starts to form around the hub and rotor, the rotor may not come off easily, so it may be necessary to use two bolts as a

puller. Install two 8mm × 12mm long (½") bolts into the rotor and turn them equally until the rotor comes off.

7 Put the new rotor on and fasten it with the retaining screw on models so equipped. Make sure it is properly aligned on the hub. Then install the caliper mount to the steering knuckle and torque these bolts to 25 foot-pounds.

CALIPER MOUNT · **ANTI-RATTLE CLIPS** · **ROTOR**

8 To install the new disc pads, simply reverse the disassembly procedure. That is, first install the anti-rattle clips into the caliper mount, being careful not to force the anti-rattle clips. Then slid the disc brake pads in against the rotor. Now install the brake shim pad (note that there is only one shim on these models) onto the outer disc brake pad.

9 Use an old brake pad and a C-clamp to push the caliper piston into its bore so the caliper will fit around the new pads. It may be necessary to open the bleed screw slightly in order for the piston to compress.

10 Swing the caliper body down over the disc brake pads, and install the lower caliper retaining pins. Then torque the upper and lower pins to 13 foot-pounds.

11 Repeat the procedure on the other front wheel and then pump the brake pedal several times until it is firm and the pads and caliper seat.

12 Now complete the final check. Check the fluid level in the master cylinder reservoir and correct, if necessary, with a high-temperature brake fluid (only DOT 3 or 4). Replace the reservoir cover, pump the brakes a few more times, and inspect for leaks.

13 Reinstall the tire-and-wheel assembly and torque the wheel lug nuts (or bolts on Preludes) to 65 foot-pounds.

14 Remove the car from the safety stands and road-test. Drive slowly at first.

Replace rear brake shoes

Rear brake shoe replacement on the Honda is easily tackled by the average do-it-yourselfer. The rear brakes on all Hondas are power-assisted with a leading-trailing shoe-and-drum arrangement. If you suspect your rear brakes are faulty and you are considering relining them (replacing the brake shoes), you should first chock the front wheels, jack up the rear of the car, place safety stands (at the point where you would normally jack up the car to change a flat tire), remove the wheel and drum, and inspect the lining. If less than .080 ($^5/_{64}$) of an inch remains, the brake shoes should be replaced. When relining the shoes, you should take the drums to your auto parts store or auto machine shop for inspection, measuring, and possibly machining. The rear brake drums must be perfectly round and smooth and must not exceed the dimension stamped on the inside of the drums.

Before replacing the brake shoes on either manual- or self-adjusting systems, check the wheel cylinders for brake fluid leaks. If there is any evidence of a leak, reassemble the brake drums and take the car to a mechanic or brake specialist for repairs.

To replace rear brake shoes on models with manual adjustment

Manually adjusted brake shoes are found on the rear of 1973–79 Civic 1200 models, 1975–79 CVCC sedan and wagon models, and 1976–80 Accord models (including the LX and four-door). Before starting the job, chock the front wheels, jack up the car, and support it on safety stands.

1 To facilitate rear brake drum removal, make sure the emergency brake is released, then back off on the adjuster bolt behind the wheel in the lower middle of the backing plate.

2 Remove the tire-and-wheel assembly.

3 Remove the bolts holding the rear wheel bearing dust cap using a 10mm wrench or socket assembly. Then remove the cotter pin from the rear axle nut and remove the nut itself.

4 Remove the drum. *CAUTION: There will be a lot of black brake dust on all the components. Do not blow this dust around and certainly don't breathe it in. It is asbestos and very dangerous.*

5 Remove the lower return spring (both models), the two small upper return springs (wagon model), and the single upper return spring (other models with manual adjustment)

Brake failure

If your brake pedal suddenly sinks all the way to the floor, pump it to build up the pressure. If this doesn't work, use your parking brake, but apply it gently so you don't lock the brakes and throw your car into a skid. Shift to a lower gear so the engine can slow you down. Finally, you can turn off the engine, leaving the car in gear, and the engine will slow you down. But if you have power steering, you may lose it when you turn off the engine.

with a pair of needlenose pliers and another suitable tool. Then remove the two brake shoe hold-down clamps by depressing and sliding them down the slot to the exit hole.

6 Remove the brake shoes without disturbing the wheel cylinder.

7 Loosen the parking brake adjuster, located between the two rear wheels, before installing the new shoes. See the instructions later in this chapter.

8 To install new rear drum brake shoes, reverse the above disassembly procedure. Make sure the upper and lower springs are properly installed. The upper spring on sedan and Accord models has the coils on the end of the spring facing outward from the brake shoes, and the lower spring on these models has the coils on the end of the spring facing inward of the brake shoes.

9 Recheck all of your work. Are the brake shoes properly seated into the adjuster, parking brake lever, and wheel cylinder activating pins? Are the springs properly installed? Using sandpaper, sand the linings lightly to remove any grease, oil stains or dirt that may have gotten on them.

10 Replace the drum, axle nut, cotter pin, dust cover, and tire-and-wheel assembly on all models.

11 Repeat the procedure on the other rear brake.

12 Pump the pedal a few times to seat the brake shoes to the drum, then adjust the brakes.

13 Check the master cylinder reservoir for proper fluid level. If necessary, add only DOT 3 or 4 heavy-duty brake fluid.

14 Remove the car from the safety stands and roadtest it. Drive slowly at first.

🛑 Install the new shoes with clean hands to avoid getting any grease on the brake linings. If grease soaks in, it can ruin a good brake job. And be careful when installing the brake shoe springs. You could hurt your hand if they slip when you're stretching them.

OR if you have a wagon model it has a slightly different spring arrangement. The two small upper springs attach outward of the shoes and the lower spring is attached inward of the shoes. The main idea is to get the wire connecting the two coils as far away from center as possible to make room for the hub.

drum. They should be installed with special driver tools. Unless they are worn or full of dirt and sand, simply add grease to the bearings and replace the grease seal if it has deteriorated.

1 Install the spring washer and the castellated nut.

2 Torque the castle nut to 80 foot-pounds and insert the cotter pin.

3 Turn the nut tighter, not looser, if the hole does not line up.

Accord models

These models (including the LX and four-door) from 1976–80 utilize a tapered roller bearing that will not hold up under the same torque as the sedans. These bearings are more easily inspected and repacked with grease.

1 Line up the washer, install the outer nut, and preload the bearing by tightening to about 18 foot-pounds of torque.

2 Back off on the nut and retighten it to only three foot-pounds of torque.

3 Install the cotter pin nut over the spindle nut, lining up the hole lines to insert the pin.

1973–79 sedans and wagons

All the sedan and wagon models from 1973–79 use ball bearings that are pressed into the

To replace rear brake shoes on models with self-adjustment

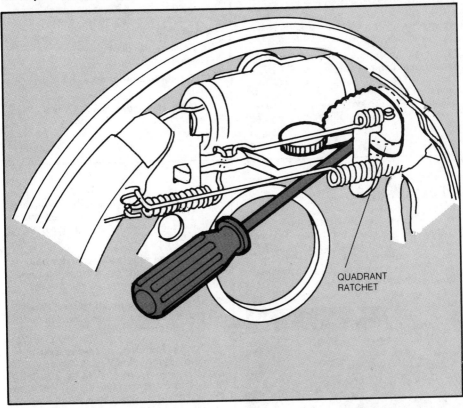

QUADRANT
RATCHET

The 1979–80 Prelude and the 1980 Civic rear brakes have a self-adjusting mechanism, but this does not make them any more difficult to work on. In fact, you follow the same procedures as for manually adjusted brakes. This shows both the proper location and direction of the springs.

1 Start by blocking the front wheels and raising them onto safety stands.

2 Release the emergency brake adjuster nut, located between the two rear wheels.

3 Carefully pry off the dust cover.

4 Remove the cotter pin and, with the proper size wrench, remove the spindle nut. The brake drum should come off. If not, you may have to use a hammer as described in the previous discussion of rear brakes with manual adjustment.

5 Before proceeding, check the wheel cylinders. If they're leaking, they should be repaired by a professional mechanic.

6 Have the drums inspected, measured, and, if necessary, machined when you reline your brakes.

7 Remove the upper and lower return springs, using a suitable tool.

8 Then remove the two brake shoe hold-down clamps by pushing them down and turning until the pin heads lines up with the slot in the clamps.

9 Reverse the disassembly procedure to install the new shoes. Note: For a more detailed explanation, follow the instructions for replacing rear brake shoes on models with manual adjustment. The biggest difference between the manual and self-adjusting brake assemblies on a Honda is the adjuster mechanism, which should be brought to its fully released position when the brakes are relined. Do this by pushing a screwdriver between the top part of the adjuster mechanism and the brake shoe where the ratchet mechanism comes through the top of the shoes.

10 Recheck all of your work. Are the brake shoes properly seated into the adjuster, parking brake lever, and wheel cylinder actuating pins? Are the springs properly installed?

11 Install the drum, outer bearing, washer, and spindle nut. The 1979–80 Prelude and the 1980 Civic models use the same type of rear drum-and-bearing assembly as the Accord models. They have tapered roller bearings and can be repacked.

12 Preload the bearing by tightening to 18 foot-pounds of torque and then back off on the nut and retorque it to only three foot-pounds.

13 Replace the dust cover and the tire-and-wheel assembly.

14 Repeat this procedure on the other rear wheel.

15 Pump the pedal, check the brake fluid level, and add fluid if necessary.

Adjust brakes

The front brakes on all Hondas are power-assisted, self-adjusting disc brakes. The rear brakes on the 1973–79 Civic 1200, the 1975–79 sedan and wagon, and the 1976–80 Accord (including the LX and four-door) all have manually adjusted rear drum brakes.

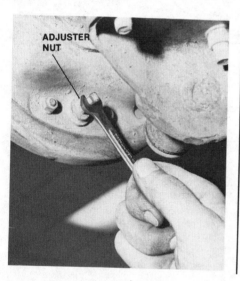

ADJUSTER NUT

1 Chock the front wheels, raise the rear wheels off the ground, and put safety stands in place. Make sure the emergency brake is released.

2 Locate the rear brake adjuster bolt, usually under a dust cover which must be replaced after adjusting the rear brakes.

3 Pump the brake pedal several times to position the shoes properly without the turning action of the drums.

4 Using a 7mm long open-end wrench, turn the adjuster bolt in a clockwise direction until the wheel locks up. Turn the adjuster counterclockwise about a half a turn. The wheel should now turn freely. If it still drags, turn the adjuster counterclockwise about another quarter turn.

The rear brakes on the 1979–80 Prelude and the 1980 Civic are self-adjusting and should adjust automatically each time the brake pedal is fully depressed. So after the rear brake drum has been serviced, pump the brakes several times and they should adjust automatically. If you suspect the brakes are not automatically adjusting, you may follow the procedures described for rear brake shoe replacement and remove the brake drum to inspect the ratchet mechanism.

PRO SHOP When doing a brake job, it's often very difficult to remove the brake drums if they haven't been off the car for some time. An effective remedy is to put a small amount of penetrating oil on the rear studs and rap the brake drum with a three- to five-pound hammer in the area between the studs. Be careful not to actually hit any of the studs. This hammering should loosen the drums enough to allow easy removal by hand.

Inspect the wheel cylinders by pulling the cylinder dust boots up before proceeding. Check to see if any fluid is visible. If you see fluid, put everything back together and take your car to a professional mechanic.

Self-adjusting brakes

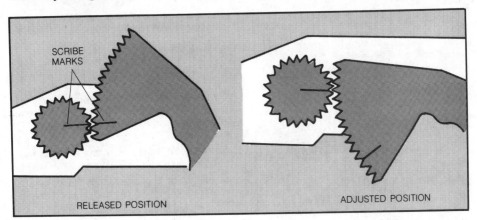

SCRIBE MARKS

RELEASED POSITION

ADJUSTED POSITION

1 Fully release the ratchet mechanism with a screwdriver and scribe the teeth that match on both the wheel and the ratchet arm.

2 Reinstall the brake drum and pump the brake pedal several times.

3 Remove the drum again and inspect the scribe marks. If they have moved, the self-adjusting mechanism is working properly.

4 If the scribe marks have not moved, reassemble the drum-and-wheel assembly, as described earlier for rear brake shoe replacement, and take your car to a professional mechanic.

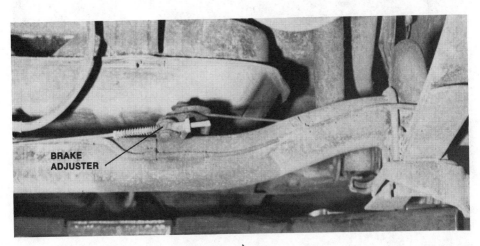

BRAKE ADJUSTER

You should not attempt to adjust the emergency brake until the rear brakes have been adjusted and are operating properly. To make this adjustment on models with self-adjusting rear brakes, pump the brake pedal several times. Make sure the front wheels are chocked and the rear of the car is securely placed on jack stands. Now pull the emergency brake lever up one click.

Note: This is a typical adjuster mechanism on a wagon. Although it may not look exactly like the adjuster on your Honda, the adjustment procedure is the same on all models.

1 Locate the emergency brake adjuster. On all Hondas, it is about half way between the two rear wheels. A more exact way of

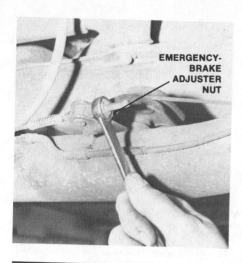

EMERGENCY-
BRAKE
ADJUSTER
NUT

finding it is to follow a wire cable from each rear wheel to where they meet at the adjuster.

2 Make sure the pivot point of the adjuster moves freely and is free of dirt and corrosion.

3 Tighten the adjusting nut by turning it clockwise until the rear wheels just start to drag when turning.

4 Release the emergency brake lever and pump the brakes several times. With the lever still released, make sure the rear wheels don't drag as they are turned.

5 If they do, back off on the adjuster nut one turn, pump the brakes, and check again.

6 Pull up on the emergency brake lever. Within three to eight clicks it should lock up the rear wheels.

How to bleed the brakes

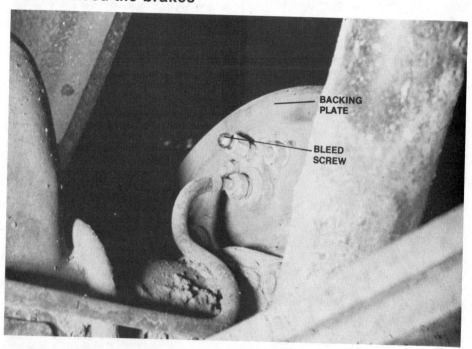

BACKING
PLATE

BLEED
SCREW

The average do-it-yourselfer would normally only get involved in brake shoe and pad replacement and brake adjustment. Neither of these jobs should require bleeding the brakes. But if the system needs bleeding, you must take your time and be very careful. Before attempting to bleed the brakes, make sure that all the connections are tight and that there are no signs of any leaks.

CAUTION: Bleeding the brakes is a difficult job and doing it wrong can result in the loss of your car and possibly your life. Before you try it, read over these instructions very carefully and make sure you completely understand them. If you have any doubts about your ability to do the job right, take your car to a professional mechanic for this repair.

If you loosen the wheel cylinders or any of the brake lines for some reason, you must bleed the brake system. Bleeding eliminates air bubbles trapped in the brake lines that can cause impaired braking and a spongy pedal. The brake system is bled by opening a small valve (called the bleed screw). On drum brakes this valve is located on the back of each wheel backing plate. On disc brakes, the bleed valve is located on the caliper where the hose enters it. When opened, this valve allows brake fluid to escape, thus removing air bubbles that are in the system.

Before starting, make sure you have an adequate supply of brake fluid and a helper. Bleeding the brakes is a two-man job unless you have a pressure bleeder. You open and close the valve at each wheel to let fluid and trapped air escape while your helper applies pressure to the brake pedal to force the fluid and air out of the system.

Bleed the brakes in the sequence shown. If your car has power brakes, start by pumping the pedal ten times, with the engine off, to use up any vacuum in the booster.

1 Jack up the car and support it on safety stands.

2 If the bleed valve has a dust cap, remove it and clean off the valve. Most professional mechanics use a pressure bleeder, which provides air-free fluid to the top filler cap of the master cylinder, but you can use a length of clean vacuum hose instead, as long as you are very careful not to let the master cylinder reservoir run dry.

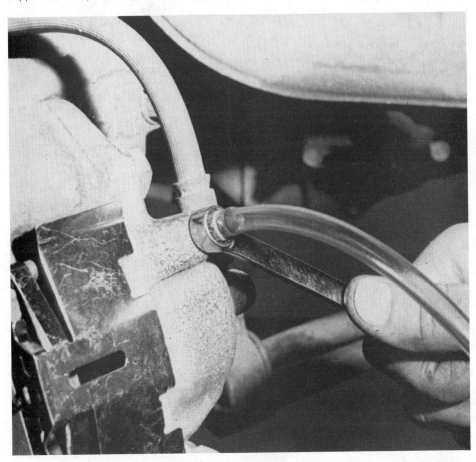

3 Attach the vacuum hose to one of the valves, and, holding the valve securely with a box wrench, insert the other end of the hose into a jar partly filled with fresh brake fluid.

4 Have your helper pump the pedal slowly several times. Then have him hold a steady pressure.

5 Open the valve three-quarters of a turn with a wrench.

6 Have your helper continue to apply the brakes slowly but steadily.

7 When the pedal reaches the floor, close the valve, then let the pedal slowly return to its normal position.

8 Repeat this procedure until air bubbles stop coming out of the hose.

9 Check the reservoir every four to five pumps, refill it to within one-half inch of the top, and replace the cover. This prevents more air from entering the system through the reservoir while you are bleeding it. If the reservoir runs dry, air will enter the system and you will have to start the whole sequence over again.

10 Bleed each wheel in this way until the old fluid runs clear.

11 Lower the car.

12 Before driving the car, start the engine and pump the brakes several times to make sure you have a firm pedal.

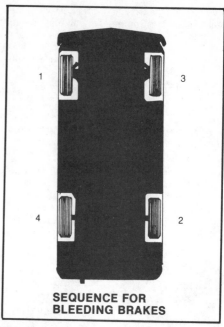

SEQUENCE FOR BLEEDING BRAKES

Should the pedal feel spongy, there is still air in the system and you must repeat the bleeding procedure.

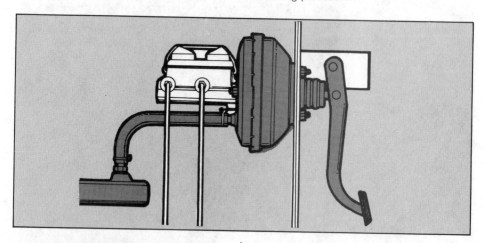

To check power brakes

Method 1

With the ignition off, pump the brake pedal several times to bleed off the vacuum in the power unit. The pedal will become firm as you pump it. Push on the pedal hard, and at the same time start the engine. If the power unit is working properly, the brake pedal should sink slightly toward the floorboard.

Method 2

A second check of the power unit can be done with a helper. Open the hood and have your helper start the engine. Listen to the power unit under the hood as your helper depresses the brake pedal and holds it down. If the power unit is working properly, you should hear a momentary hiss coming from it. If the unit continues to hiss steadily, it is defective, and only a qualified mechanic or brake specialist should repair or replace it.

About machining drums and rotors

All Honda rotors are of the single-plane type, so they are not as thick as rotors on other makes. Therefore, machining Honda rotors may take them below their minimum acceptable thickness and all Honda rotors (except those on 1979–80 Preludes and 1980 Civics) are pressed with the hub into the front wheel bearings. So the front bearings and rotor require special equipment for removal.

There are a few machine shops that can machine the rotor. However, this requires removing the rotor assembly (rotor, hub, and spindle) from the car, which is almost out of the question for the average do-it-yourselfer. So it is better to take your car to a qualified mechanic or a brake specialist to change the rotor.

To have the rear brake drums machined by a machine shop or auto parts house, mark the drums RR (right rear) and LR (left

rear) to insure that the drums are returned to the proper location on the car. Also, using a tool, make sure the drum dimensions do not exceed what is stamped inside the drum.

About brake pads

Brake pad material must pass tests that measure, among other things, its ability to grip as it should when the brakes get hot. Brake pads made by large, name-brand manufacturers will show markings stamped into the edges of the friction materials to this effect. A set of sub-standard disc brake pads might perform adequately in normal city driving, for example, but fail when they heat up trying to slow a loaded car on a long downhill run.

PRO SHOP Brake fluid is poisonous. It also damages paint. If you drain the fluid from the system or bleed the brakes, dispose of the containers you used for the job. Brake fluid also deteriorates with time. Buy one pint, keep it tightly capped, and discard it at the end of a year if it has been opened. It attracts moisture which, if introduced into the brake system, can cause corrosion and brake failure. If the label on a can of brake fluid does not say "meets MUSS No. 116, DOT 4 specifications," it probably has been packaged by a distributor who has not tested it to make sure it meets minimum US Department of Transportation standards.

PRO SHOP When you have finished bleeding the brakes on 1976 and older models, you will find the brake warning light on the dashboard lit. The light can only be turned off by centering the detented rod inside the pressure differential switch, which is a tedious procedure. You can save yourself a lot of trouble by replacing the light switch with a small threaded stud (sold in auto parts stores) before you start bleeding. Then you can replace the stud when you are finished with the job.

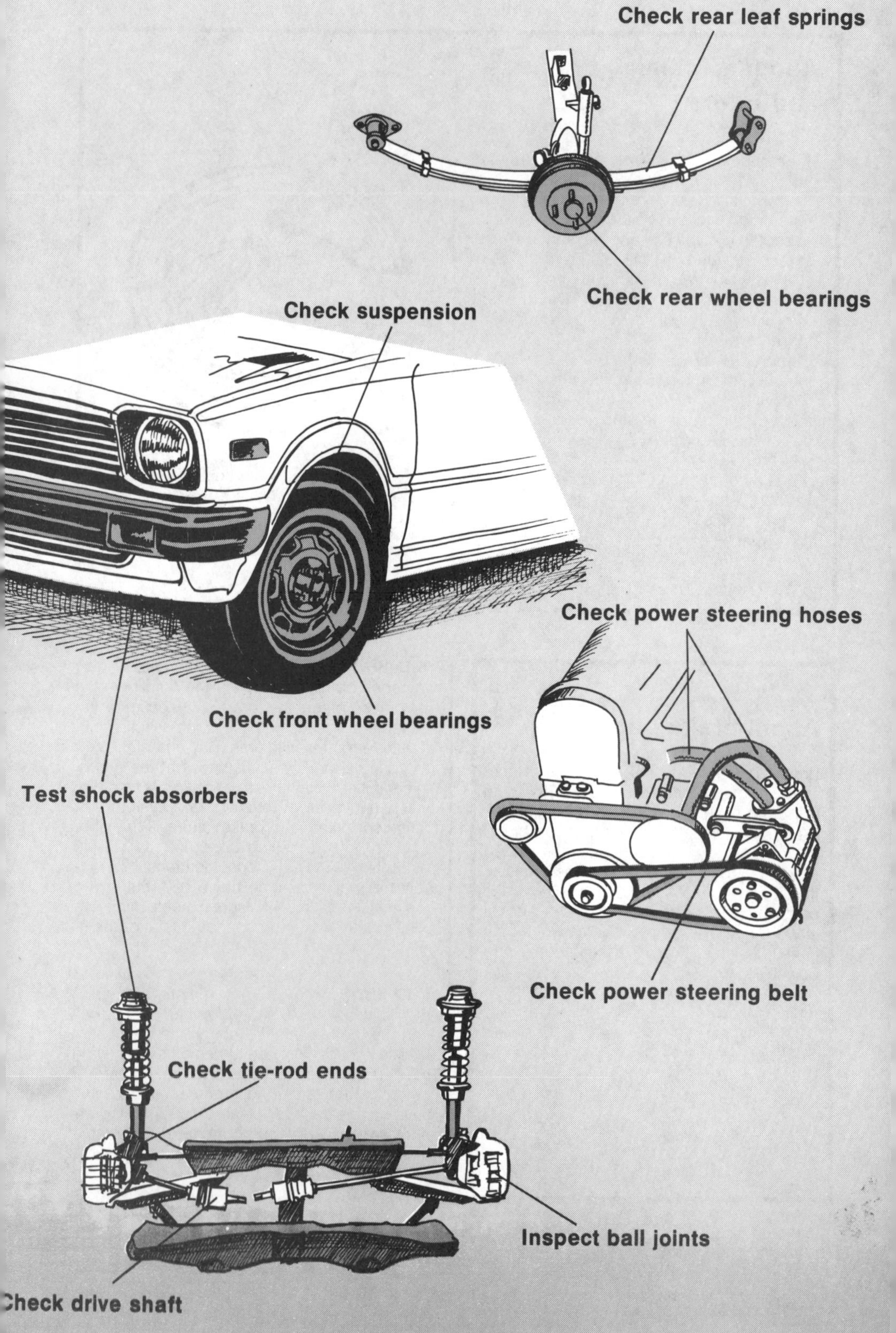

Check rear leaf springs

Check rear wheel bearings

Check suspension

Check power steering hoses

Check front wheel bearings

Test shock absorbers

Check power steering belt

Check tie-rod ends

Inspect ball joints

Check drive shaft

14

Suspension and Steering Service

1 **Check suspension.** Check for noise, steering play, instability on the road, wandering or shimmying, difficulty in steering or pulling to one side or the other. If you find any of these conditions, you could have a front end problem, perhaps just loose bushings or maybe something more serious such as excessive wear on major front end parts (p. 154).

2 **Test shock absorbers.** Use the bounce test or check for leaks or looseness and note the ride height of your car (p. 156).

3 **Check front wheel bearings.** The front wheel bearings on a Honda are of the ball-bearing type with no maintenance required other than checking and replacement when necessary. Replacement should be done by a professional (p. 158).

4 **Check rear wheel bearings.** The rear bearings are ball bearings or tapered roller bearings. Both types found on the rear are serviceable and replaceable by a do-it-yourself mechanic (p. 159).

5 **Inspect ball joints.** Hondas have only lower ball joints, which are part of the lower control arm. They must be replaced as a unit if ball joint play is excessive (162).

6 **Check tie-rod ends.** Check the tie-rod ends and tie-rod end ball joints and replace if necessary (p. 162).

7 **Check rear leaf springs.** On wagons from 1975–80, check the springs and replace if necessary. On all other models, this is a job for a professional mechanic (163).

8 **Check drive shaft.** If inspection reveals a split dust boot or a bent axle shaft, take your car to a professional mechanic (p. 164).

9 **Check power steering belt.** Inspect the tension and condition of the power steering pump belt and adjust or replace as necessary (p. 165).

10 **Check power steering hoses.** The Honda power steering system is very complex, but the do-it-yourselfer can check, and if necessary replace, the power steering hoses (p. 165).

11 **Check suspension.** On all Hondas, there are alignment specifications for the front, and for the rear on all models expect 1975–80 wagons. If your car's front or rear toe angle does not meet specifications, adjust it. If your check reveals further problems, see a professional mechanic (p. 166).

TOOLS

Essential. Basic tools • Floor jack • Safety stands • Pry bar • Ball joint separation tool Drift punch • Flare wrenches.
Handy. Fender cover • Belt tension gauge Flashlight or droplight • Clean rags or towels Creeper • Drain pan.

Check suspension

The shock absorber is one of the most important suspension components on the car. The shock affects handling, steering control, and tire wear. On the Honda, the shock is part of the MacPherson strut/coil spring assembly. A shock absorber in poor condition can cause noise in the front end, front wheel shimmy, wandering or instability, or make the car pull to one side or the other when not braking. If any of these conditions are noticed, test the shock absorbers and replace them if necessary.

Loose wheel bearings may also account for many suspension problems, especially the front wheel bearings. Loose or worn front wheel bearings can cause noise in the front end as well as vibrations, wheel shimmy, and instability. If the front wheel bearings are bad and need replacement, it will have to be done by a professional mechanic, because these bearings are pressed into the spindle. Loose rear wheel bearings may also account for some handling problems and some noise or rumbling coming from the rear. The rear wheel bearings can be replaced by the average do-it-yourselfer.

Worn ball joints can cause looseness and noise in the front end. If the ball joint lacks lubricant, it can cause hard or tight steering.

Stabilizer and/or radius (strut) rod bushings can cause noise in the front end if they're loose, especially when stopping or taking off rapidly. They can also account for front wheel shimmy and instability or wandering.

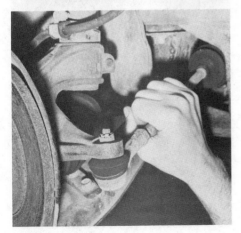

Loose or worn tie-rod ends can be critically detrimental to the overall handling and steering response of the car.

WATER PUMP PULLEY

POWER STEERING PUMP PULLEY

A poorly operating power steering system, caused by a loose or worn belt or a loose rack, could contribute to erratic operation, front wheel shimmy, and wandering.

Incorrect front or rear wheel alignment may cause front wheel shimmy, instability, wandering, hard steering or the car pulling to one side or the other when not braking.

Test shock absorbers

Honda shock absorbers are part of the Mac-Pherson strut/coil spring assembly, which comprises part of the independent suspension on all four wheels, except on the rear of the wagon. The rear of the wagon utilizes a conventional-type shock.

If your car seems unstable on the road, you should test your shock absorbers. Indications of instability include feeling road shocks, up-and-down bobbing of the car for a long time after hitting a bump, or a general lack of control in handling. Also, any clunking sounds from beneath the car when it hits a bump or makes a turn should lead you to suspect worn shocks. Deterioration of shocks is gradual; they don't go bad all at once. Therefore, drivers are seldom aware of the subtle changes in vehicle handling caused by weakened shock absorbers. Since a potentially dangerous situation can develop without your being aware of it, you should take a few minutes every six months to test your shocks.

Shock absorbers fail in three ways

1 The seal cover that is supposed to keep hydraulic fluid inside the lower cylinder deteriorates and hydraulic fluid is lost.

2 The parts mounting the shock firmly at the top and bottom cylinders, more often at the bottom, wear excessively and loosen. This causes the shock to wobble. A shock absorber that has side-play cannot damp properly and causes instability.

3 Internal parts, such as the piston and various springs, wear excessively. This reduces shock damping capability. Of the three types of damage, this one takes the longest to occur.

To test shocks for wear

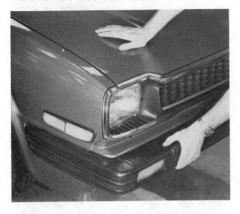

1 Park the car on level pavement, then turn off the engine. Note: You do not need any tools to test your shocks.

2 Set the parking brake firmly. If your car has an automatic transmission, set it in Park. If it has a manual transmission, set it in gear.

3 Stand at any corner of the car, place your hands on the bumper or fender and press down with as much force as you can muster. When the corner reaches its maximum downward point, let up. Keep doing this until the car is rocking up and down.

4 While the car is rocking on a downward stroke, and the corner has been pushed to its maximum point, quickly remove your hands from the bumper or fender. If the car's body comes up one time and settles level, the shock absorber in that corner is probably OK. If the body bounces up and down again, that is, if it keeps bouncing instead of settling level and in a smooth manner, the shock absorber in that corner is weak.

5 Perform this test at each of your car's other three corners.

To test for loose shock bushings

1 Jack up and support the rear of the car.

2 Grasp the shock absorber with your hand and twist it from side to side while checking the bushings for excessive movement.

3 Replace the shock if the bushings are worn.

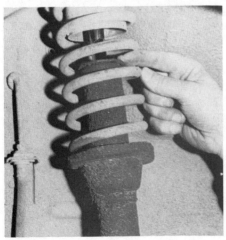

To check shocks for leaks

1 Jack up and support the car.

2 Visually check the lower section of the shock for fluid leaks

3 Replace the shock if a leak is detected.

To replace wagon shock absorbers

Shock replacement can be performed by the average do-it-yourselfer on the rear of the 1975–80 wagon because this model has a conventional absorber, not the newer MacPherson strut assembly.

1 Chock the front wheels and raise the rear wheels, but not off the ground. Support the car with safety stands.

2 Remove the upper and then the lower shock mounting bolt.

3 Remove the old shock absorber and replace it with a new one by reversing the removal procedure.

4 Make sure the bushings are in place and the mounting bolts are tightened to about 32 foot-pounds of torque.

Check front wheel bearings

1 Chock the rear wheels and jack up and support the front end of the car on safety stands. Note: Have a helper ready for the next step.

2 Grasp the bottom of one front tire with your left hand. With your right hand, grasp the top, then pull out at the bottom while simultaneously pushing in at the top. Have your helper watch the inner part of the wheel.

3 If there is play in the inner wheel area or if you notice a rumbling sound when you rotate either front wheel, you should take your car to a qualified mechanic to have the front wheel bearings replaced. Working on this assembly requires special tools and skills.

About MacPherson struts

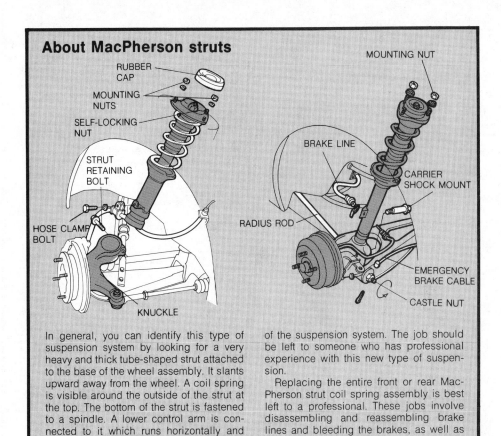

In general, you can identify this type of suspension system by looking for a very heavy and thick tube-shaped strut attached to the base of the wheel assembly. It slants upward away from the wheel. A coil spring is visible around the outside of the strut at the top. The bottom of the strut is fastened to a spindle. A lower control arm is connected to it which runs horizontally and attaches to the frame. The shock absorber is inside the tubular strut. You cannot replace the shock without disassembling part of the suspension system. The job should be left to someone who has professional experience with this new type of suspension.

Replacing the entire front or rear MacPherson strut coil spring assembly is best left to a professional. These jobs involve disassembling and reassembling brake lines and bleeding the brakes, as well as other disconnecting and reconnecting procedures which are quite complicated.

Check rear wheel bearings

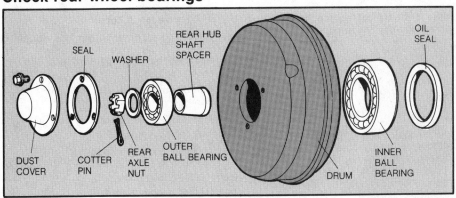

This rear wheel bearing assembly with ball bearings is typical of 1973–79 Civic 1200 and 1975–79 CVCC sedan and wagon models. The rear wheel bearings can be checked the same way as the front wheel bearings but, unlike the front bearings, the rear ones are serviceable by the do-it-yourselfer.

1 If you suspect a rear wheel bearing failure, take the dust cover off the drum by removing the three 10mm bolts.

2 Remove the cotter pin and the rear axle nut.

3 Remove the rear drum. It may be necessary to back off the rear brake adjuster and, in stubborn cases, to tap carefully with a hammer between the studs.

4 If further inspection indicates the bearings must be replaced, the old ones must be driven out with a drift punch, alternating back and forth so you don't destroy the bore the bearing rides in.

5 Carefully install the new bearings with a

tool (such as a large socket), contacting the outer bearing race but not interfering with the hub. When installing new bearings, make sure the spacer is in place between the bearings (with the smaller end facing outward) before the other bearing is installed.

6 Install a new oil seal on the inside bearing and install the drum.

7 Torque the rear axle nut to about 80 foot-pounds, install a new cotter pin, and replace the dust cover.

8 Adjust the rear brakes and install the tire-and-wheel assembly.

9 Repeat this procedure on the other side.

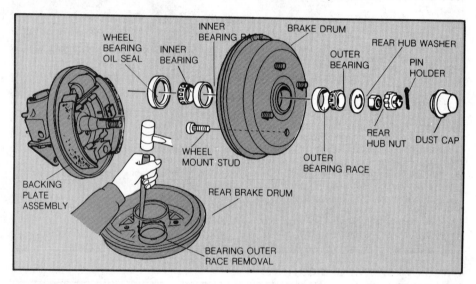

Here is the typical wheel bearing arrangement with tapered roller-type ball bearings found on the rear of the 1976–79 Accords, 1979 Preludes, and all 1980 model Hondas.

1 Chock the front wheel and jack up and support the rear wheel. Note: Have a helper ready.

2 Test the bearing by grasping the wheel at the top and bottom and pushing in and out while your helper watches the inner wheel movement. If the wheel assembly is moving in and out, this may indicate a faulty rear wheel bearing, and further diagnosis is necessary.

3 Remove the tire-and-wheel assembly.

4 Pull off the spindle nut dust cover (you may have to work the cover off carefully with a screwdriver).

5 Remove the cotter pin and spindle nut.

6 Pull the rear drum about half-way out toward you, then push it back in place. The outer bearing should stay on the spindle shaft or at least be loose from the hub.

7 Remove the bearings and make a closer inspection.

8 Pull the drum all the way off and remove the inner bearing for inspection.

9 Remove the inner bearing by placing the drum on a clean surface with the lugs facing up.

10 Put a wood dowel, such as an old broomstick cut to about 12 inches long, through the outer bearing opening in the drum and against the inner bearing, using a hammer.

11 Strike the dowel with the hammer to

release the inner bearing and the grease seal. Note direction of grease seal lip for proper reassembly.

12 Replace the bearing races (which are pressed into the hub) if the bearings are to be replaced. Drive the old races out using a drift punch and hammer. Alternate back and forth to keep the bearing race from becoming cocked in the hub.

13 Install the new bearing race using a suitable tool or large socket of the same outer dimension as the race to avoid scoring the bearing surface.

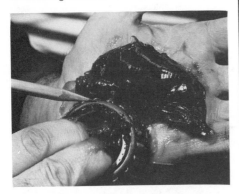

14 Grease the bearings if they do not come pre-packed with grease. To do this, first take the larger bearing in one hand, then place a small amount of wheel bearing grease on the palm of your other hand. Force the grease through the bearing until it oozes out of the opposite sides. Repeat this operation until you have forced grease into the entire bearing by working your way around its circumference. Place the bearing on a clean surface.

15 Repeat the above operation on the outer bearing—the smaller one.

16 Install the inner bearing with the taper facing the inside of the drum.

17 Install a new grease seal, but use only a grease seal installer or you may split the lip on the seal. The wiper edge or lip of the seal must face the bearing. Apply a very small amount of grease to the lip.

🛑 Be sure the inside of the brake drum is completely free of grease. Grease in this area will cause braking problems.

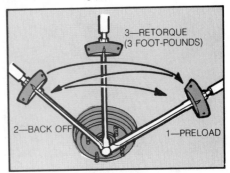

3—RETORQUE (3 FOOT-POUNDS)
2—BACK OFF
1—PRELOAD

18 To reassemble, simply reverse the disassembly procedure. Carefully replace the brake drum onto the spindle. Then install the outer bearing, the tongue washer, and the axle nut. Make sure you preload the axle nut by tightening it to about 18 foot-pounds. Now back off on the nut and torque it to only about three foot-pounds.

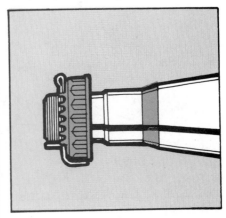

19 Secure the cotter pin with a pair of diagonal pliers. Spread the pin ends that protrude down past the nut, pulling one end toward yourself. Bend the other end back towards the tongue washer.

20 Replace the dust cover using a rubber mallet, then replace the tire-and-wheel assembly. Finally, lower the car, check the brakes, and adjust them if necessary.

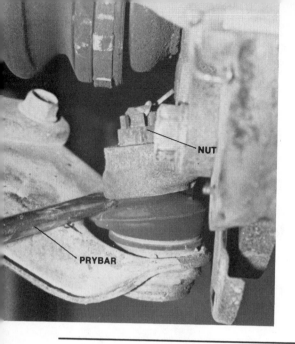

NUT

PRYBAR

Inspect ball joints

1 Jack up and support the front end of the car on safety stands.

2 Remove the front tire-and-wheel assembly.

3 Visually inspect the ball joint boot for deterioration, splits, and excessive dirt. You can also insert a pry bar between the steering knuckle and the lower control arm and move the bar up and down while watching for play in the ball joint. If there is measurable movement in the joint or if dirt has gotten into it from a bad boot, the joint should be replaced.

4 To replace a ball joint, you should take your car to a qualified mechanic or front-end specialist, since the job requires special tools and skills. The lower ball joint on a Honda is part of the lower control arm and when the lower control arm is replaced, both caster and camber can be affected.

Check tie-rod ends

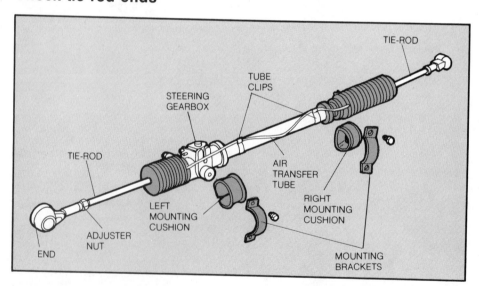

TIE-ROD

STEERING GEARBOX

TUBE CLIPS

TIE-ROD

AIR TRANSFER TUBE

LEFT MOUNTING CUSHION

RIGHT MOUNTING CUSHION

END

ADJUSTER NUT

MOUNTING BRACKETS

1 Jack up and support the front end of the car.

2 Grasp the tie-rod and pull it up and down, while observing the tie-rod end ball joint where it fits into the steering arm. If the tie-rod end ball joint has play or if the tie-rod is bent, they must be replaced.

To replace tie-rod ends

1 Locate the tie-rod end and count the number of threads exposed on the tie-rod up to the lock nut. Record this number for correct reinstallation of the new tie-rod end.

2 Spray the tie-rod lock nut and the tie-rod castellated nut with penetrating oil.

3 Remove the cotter pin from the castellated nut and loosen the nut about four or five turns, but do not remove it yet.

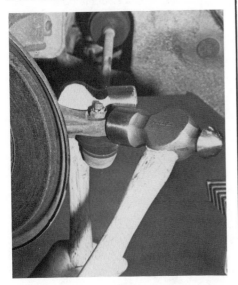

4 Hold a heavy ball peen hammer against the back side of the steering arm, directly behind the area where the tie-rod end fits into the arm.

5 With a second ball peen hammer, strike the steering arm with a sharp, heavy blow,

but be careful not to hit the tie-rod end ball joint boot or stud. This should release the tie-rod end. Several attempts may be required to free a more stubborn tie-rod end.

6 When the end is free, remove the castellated nut, loosen the tie-rod lock nut, and turn the tie-rod end off, counting the number of turns to remove it. Record this number to ensure correct installation of the new tie-rod end.

7 Install the new tie-rod end onto the tie-rod, screwing the end on only the number of turns it took to remove the old one. This should leave the same number of threads showing as were exposed when you began the job.

8 Insert the tie-rod end into the steering arm, then reinstall the castellated nut and torque to 25 foot-pounds.

9 Put in the new cotter pin. If the pin access hole in the tie-rod end does not line up, tighten the nut just until the hole is exposed. Tighten the tie-rod lock nut to 33 foot-pounds.

10 Repeat this operation on the other tie-rod end if there is any play or the tie-rod end is worn. When you have completed this job, you must have your front wheels checked for alignment, especially for toe. This must be done by an auto mechanic or a front-end specialist with wheel alignment equipment.

Check rear leaf springs

This three semi-elleptic leaf-spring arrangement is a typical one found on the rear of 1975–80 Honda wagons. This is the only rear leaf spring arrangement the do-it-yourselfer can work on. The rear springs on

all other Hondas are part of the independent MacPherson strut coil spring assembly and only a professional mechanic can work on them.

A sagging, tail-dragging ride, bottoming out when going over bumps or road dips with a normal passenger load, or an uneven ride height can be signs of a weak leaf spring on the rear of a wagon, though leaf springs on the rear of a Honda wagon don't often need to be replaced.

CAUTION: You will be working very close to the brake lines. Be very careful not to hit or exert force against these lines.

To replace rear leaf spring on 1975–80 wagons

1 Chock the front wheels, jack up the rear, and support the car on safety stands.

2 Remove the rear wheel to get access to the spring.

3 Place a floor jack under the axle and raise it just enough to take the weight off the springs.

4 Remove the bolt from the bottom mounting bracket of the shock absorber.

5 Remove the front spring mounting nut and then the bolt assembly.

6 Loosen the rear shockle bolt.

7 Remove the nuts from the U bolts holding the leaf spring to the axle. As you loosen the nuts, the spring will start to drop.

8 Remove the rear shockle.

9 To install the new leaf spring, reverse the removal procedure, making sure all spring bushings are also new and in place. Also make sure all mounting bolts are tight.

10 Repeat this procedure on the other side in order to maintain equal ride height and ride stability.

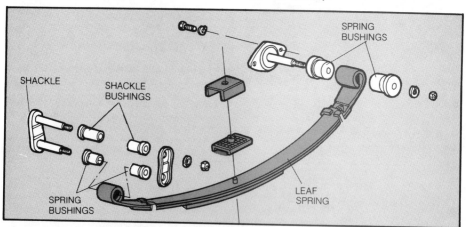

Check drive shaft

Each drive shaft assembly consists of two constant velocity joints. One joint is not serviceable and neither requires maintenance other than inspection. If you notice upon inspection that one of the dust boots has a split or if one of the axle shafts is bent, you should take your car to a professional mechanic because the replacement procedure is complex and requires special skills.

Check power steering belt

Power steering is standard only on 1978–80 Accord LX models and 1979–80 Accord 4-door models. Visually inspect the power steering belt for cracks, cuts, fraying or severe glazing. If you find any of these conditions or if the pump adjusting bolt reaches the hump in the top of the adjusting arm, the belt must be replaced.

To replace the power steering belt

1 To replace the power steering belt on a Honda, you do not have to remove any other engine belt if it is the only faulty one, since this belt is the outside belt. However, the working quarters for replacing the belt are close, so you must loosen the adjuster belt and the pump pivot bolt in order to move the top of the power steering pump as close to the engine as possible. Note: The pump may not move close enough to the engine to remove the belt.

2 Work the old belt off the engine crank pulley, if necessary.

3 Install the new belt on the pump first, then work it onto the engine crank pulley.

4 If you install a new belt or if the old belt is loose, but in good shape, you must adjust it. There should be only about $9/16$-inch deflection in the belt between the two pullies, and for a new belt there should be less than $1/2$-inch.

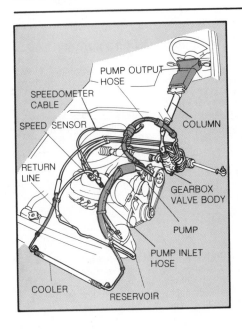

Check power steering hoses

The Honda power steering system is a variable-assist type. The degree of assistance is determined mostly by road speed and to a lesser extent by load. The system is controlled by a speed sensor located at the transmission, and the system can generate pressures in excess of 1000 psi, so there is a power steering fluid cooler. Since all the sub-components of this system are located in different areas of the engine compartment, there are numerous power steering pressure hoses. Since the power steering system is so complex, you should limit your work to checking and replacing hoses. If you suspect further problems, you should take your car to a professional mechanic.

1 Check the power steering hoses for leaks and carefully identify which hose(s), if any, are faulty.

🛑 The pressure line connections at the steering gearbox assembly should be removed by jacking up the car and supporting it on jack stands, then removing the metal shield protecting the gearbox assembly. Be sure to identify the proper connection.

2 Place a small drain pan directly under the point at which the hose connects. Note: Try to remove only one hose at a time, and always route the hose back in the same way that it came off.

🛑 If one of the pressure lines is leaking, make sure the replacement hose is capable of withstanding the same pressures. Most of the pressure lines are steel and should be replaced with the same type, which have double-flared ends.

3 Loosen and remove the pressure hose fitting from the pump with the proper size flare nut wrench. At this point, fluid will drain out of the pump and into the drain pan.

4 Remove the other end of the pressure hose from the steering gearbox assembly with the correct size flare nut wrench.

5 Install the new pressure hose at the gearbox assembly, starting the fittings by hand and tightening them securely. Note: These removal and installation procedures apply to all power steering hoses, although some hoses are secured by clamps rather than by tightening the fittings by hand.

6 Remove the reservoir dipstick and fill the reservoir with fluid.

🛑 Use only Honda power steering fluid. Other fluids are not completely compatible with the Honda system and they have a deteriorating effect on seals.

7 Start the engine, turn the steering wheel from full-left to full-right lock several times, switch the engine off, and recheck the fluid level.

8 Check all connections for leaks.

Check suspension

Either front or rear misalignment can cause such conditions as front wheel shimmy, instability or wandering, hard steering or pulling to one side or the other while cruising.

There are basic caster, camber, and toe-out specifications for the front of all Honda models from 1973–80. There are also camber and toe specifications for the rear of these models (except for wagons from 1975–80). However, only front and rear toe are adjustable. If any other suspension angles don't meet specifications, it is usually an indication of a worn, bent or failed suspension component, and the condition should be checked by a professional mechanic or front-end specialist.

To check tires and springs

Some suspension-related problems you can correct yourself. Others must be left to a professional mechanic or front-end specialist. You can avoid aggravating existing problems and save money by correcting those things which are within the scope of the do-it-yourselfer. The following conditions may appear on any of the tires of a Honda with four-wheel independent suspension.

WEAR WEAR

Underinflation of the tires causes the edges of the tread to wear more rapidly than the center. Inflate the tires to the manufacturer's specifications, which are indicated on the driver's door.

Overinflation of the tires causes the center of the tread to wear more rapidly than the edge. Reduce the tire pressure to the manufacturer's specifications.

Out-of-balance wheels or faulty suspension alignment may cause uneven or spotty tread wear, which sometimes takes the form of cupping, scalloping or bald spots around the tire. In any case, see a front-end specialist.

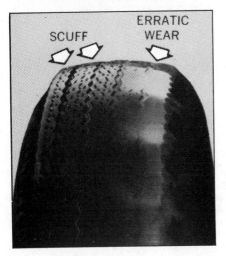

Tread with one side worn off on a front tire is caused by improper camber setting. Correction requires a front-end specialist.

MAXIMUM SCUFF AREA

Tiny feathered edges on one side of the tread block indicate excessive toe-in. If you place the palm of your hand on the tread and move it inward, the tire may feel smooth. As you pull your hand outward, you will feel sharp edges. See a front-end specialist for this problem.

HEAVY WEAR + DEPRESSIONS
WEAR + DEPRESSIONS

The wear pattern resulting from toe-out is the reverse of that caused by toe-in. Take your car to a front-end specialist.

Bars appear once the tire tread is worn down to $1/6$-inch. They appear as smooth bands running across the tread area. When bands appear in two or more adjacent grooves, the tire is at the end of its safe useful life and should be replaced.

To check tire pressure

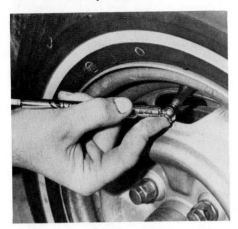

Checking tire pressure is about the easiest item for anyone to check, but most people seem to ignore it. Tire pressure should be checked at least once a month when the tire is cold (not driven recently). Maintaining proper tire pressure and careful driving will help prevent most tire damage.

Proper tire pressure and balance can also reduce suspension wear. This is because an improperly inflated tire changes alignment angles, which puts more stress and strain on the suspension components, thereby reducing their longevity. Likewise, an improperly balanced tire which goes uncorrected produces excessive vibration and wear on suspension components.

To check spring height

Check the front and rear spring height by measuring from the side marker light to the ground. This may reveal a possible suspension problem which, if left uncorrected, could cause other suspension problems. Although there are spring height specifications, they are too numerous to mention for each model. The important thing is that you have equality from side to side. More than half an inch variation indicates a possible problem. Front to rear will not be equal. Take your car to a professional mechanic or front-end specialist if you suspect a problem here.

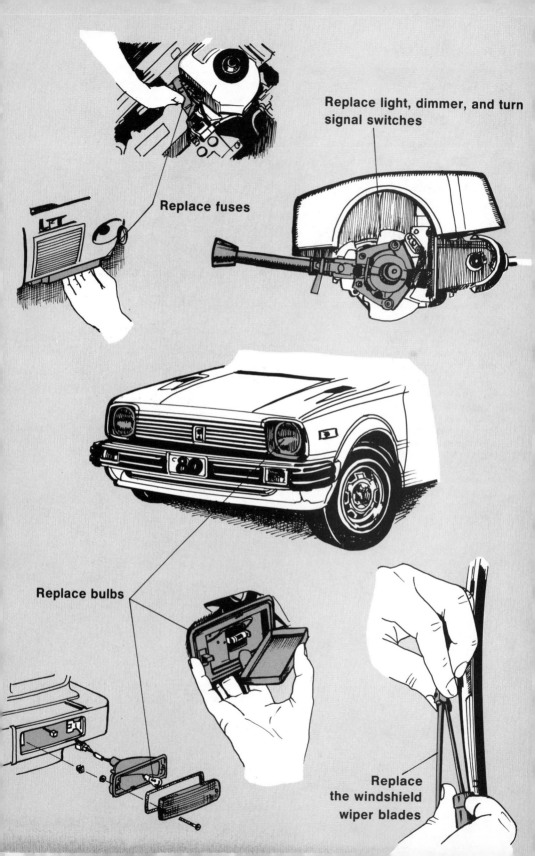

Replace light, dimmer, and turn signal switches

Replace fuses

Replace bulbs

Replace the windshield wiper blades

15

Electrical System Service

PREP: Make sure the battery is fully charged and the charging system is working properly.

1 Replace fuses. Whether you are tracing some electrical problem or if you just want to replace a fuse, you need to know where the fuse box is for your model Honda and you must know how to find out whether the burnt fuse is really your problem (p. 172).

2 Replace bulbs. Most of the safety-related (headlamp, stop, turn signal, etc.) light bulbs can be easily replaced (p. 175).

3 Replace light, dimmer, and turn signal switches. All of these switches are part of a combination switch, so if one fails, the entire switch must be replaced. The windshield wiper/washer switch is attached to this combination switch and can also be easily removed (p. 181).

4 Replace the windshield wiper blades. Smearing or streaking of the windows with the wipers could mean the wiper blades need replacement (p. 181).

Essential. Basic tools • Test light • Fuse puller • Electric drill • ¼-inch bit.
Handy. Voltmeter • Ohmmeter • Rubber hammer • Center punch.

Replace fuses

To replace main fuse

1 Locate the main fuse near the battery.
On 1973–79 Civic 1200s and 1975–79 CVCC sedans and wagons, the main fuse is attached to the wheel well behind the battery just above the voltage regulator. On 1976–80 Preludes and 1980 Civics, the main fuse is located between the battery and the shock tower next to the battery.

2 To replace the main fuse, unscrew the two retaining screws and remove the old fuse parts.

3 Install a new fuse of equal amperage (35, 45 or 55 amp) to the fuse removed.

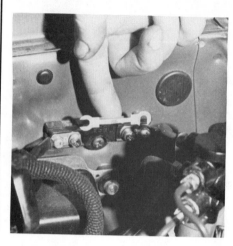

Tips on electrical service

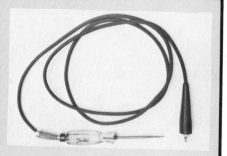

• If you suspect an electrical problem, first check the fuse box for a blown or defective fuse.

• Remember: You could have a bad fuse without a visible separation of the fuse filament.

• To check the condition of a bulb quickly, hold it up to the light and tap it with your finger. If the filament or shreds of the filament shake around inside, replace the bulb.

• When inserting a bulb into its socket, make sure there is a good contact between the bulb itself and the contact strip in the socket.

• If the bulb goes on and off when shaken lightly, you are getting poor contact between the bulb and the socket. Take out the bulb and reinsert it to get better contact.

• All parking and side marker lights have a sealing rubber gasket behind the lens. When replacing bulbs behind these lenses, be careful not to rip the gasket. If you do, replace it. Otherwise, the whole assembly can fill up with water and short out the bulb. *CAUTION. Be very careful when changing fuses. They break easily and the glass*

particles can cut you. Also be careful when inserting a light bulb into its socket.

• The test light is probably one of the most useful and easy-to-use tools for locating an electrical problem. To use one, simply attach the alligator clip to a good ground, such as a steering column bolt. Using the painted part of the tester, carefully probe the suspected failed component to see if there is voltage available. This is indicated by a light in the tester going on if voltage is available. If voltage is available to a nonfunctioning component, this is a good indication of a failed component. First, make sure the suspected unit has a good ground (usually a separate back wire on most Honda components).

To replace other fuses

1 Locate the fuse box. The fuse box on 1973–79 Civic 1200s and 1975–79 CVCC sedans and wagons is in the upper part of the kick panel on the passenger side. To open the fuse box, just squeeze on the right side and open from right to left. The Accord models (including LX and four-door),

1976–80, and 1979–80 Preludes have the fuse box located on the opposite side of the car to the left of the steering column as part of the lower dash. To gain access to the fuses, push in and pull down.

OR if you own a 1980 Civic, it is equipped with a fuse panel similar in location to the Prelude, but with an access cover that pulls out and exposes the fuses. The panel is to the left of the steering column as part of the lower dash, and is marked "fuse box."

2 With the ignition switch turned off, remove the fuse with a fuse puller (many assorted fuse kits contain a fuse puller). If you do not have one, the fuse can be pried out by using half a clothespin. Use firm, steady pressure to remove it without breaking it.

3 Position the new fuse against the retaining clips, then press both ends of the fuse inward against the clips until the fuse snaps into place.

4 Check the operation of the circuit for which the fuse was replaced. If the fuse burns, there is a short in the circuit and you should have it checked by a professional mechanic. Note: A short circuit is typically caused by the insulation on a wire rubbing through until the wire contacts the metal body of the car, which is grounded, thus causing a short in the wiring. There may also be an internal electrical problem in one of the components in the circuit that keeps burning the fuses.

5 If you notice several components not functioning, check to see if the fuse is burned. If so, and a replaced fuse also burns, you may disconnect the components in that circuit and put another fuse in the fuse holder. If this fuse burns, you either missed one of the components in the circuit or one of the wires is shorted and should be repaired by a professional mechanic. If the fuse does not burn, reconnect one component at a time until the fuse burns and you will have located the defective part of the circuit. Further diagnosis is necessary and would require a wiring diagram. Because of the complexity and the number of Honda models, it is impossible to include all of them in this book. Also, the system, the circuits, and the testing can get very involved, so it is a problem best left to an expert.

ECONOTIP Does it seem like a lot of trouble to fill the tank every time you get gas and figure the mileage? It may be easier to just dash into a station without a line and pump in a few gallons. But that technique may ultimately consume more gas. If the mileage is checked every tankful, it will be obvious when something goes wrong with the engine and the mileage starts to fall off. You may not even notice that the car is running differently, but the falling mileage will prove that something is wrong. If you are really serious about getting the best mileage, check it with every fillup, and also check the engine (or the driver) whenever the mileage gets worse.

Fuse data

All Hondas are equipped with a main fuse of either 35 amp (for the Prelude Sun Roof), 45 amp (for the 1973–79 Civic 1200 models) or 55 amp (for 1975–79 CVCC sedans and wagons, 1976–80 Accords, 1979–80 Preludes, and 1980 Civics). This is a special fuse that looks like a small wrench. Hondas also use the tubetype fuse of 10 amp, 15 amp, and recently of 20 amp. You should replace a fuse with the same amperage rating as the one removed. A fuse of higher rating could cause severe wire harness or component damage.

All Hondas have fuse identification labels over the fuses or in the fuse box cover. These can be used as quick references to help identify the fuses.

You can also identify the fuses and the main components they control by using the following charts.

This fuse box is similar to the ones found on 1973–79 Civic 1200 models and 1975–79 CVCC sedan and wagon models, except the 1974–75 Civic 1200, which has two more fuses for the seat-belt interlock system.

CODE NO.	FUSE SIZE	MAIN COMPONENTS
1	10A	Fuel pump (not on Civic 1200's), voltage regulator, carburetor solenoids, fan relay
2	10A	Wiper and washer front (and rear if so equipped)
3	10A	Turn signals, backup lights, gauges, (fuel and temperature)
4	15A	Heater blower, radio, rear window defroster
5	15A	Stoplights, hazard relay, horns
6	10A	Cigar lighter, interior lights
7	15A	Dash lights, taillights, marker lights, license lights
8	15A	Headlights
(9)	(10A)	(Interlock system—1974 and 1975 Civic 1200's only)
(10)	(10A)	(Interlock seat switch—1975 and 1975 Civic 1200's only)

Replace bulbs

All cars are equipped with a variety of lights, each of which performs a specific function. The major lights you'll find on your car include headlights (some models have two sets, one for low beams and one for high), and parking, backup, tail, brake, and side marker lights. In addition, some models have auxiliary lighting for interiors, dash gauges, and trunk and hatch compartments. Headlights are of the sealed-beam type. That is, you can't remove the bulb alone. You must remove and replace the entire unit including the lens and reflector. You can check all your car lights in less than a minute with a helper outside the car.

1 Turn on the headlights. On dim (low beam), two of the four sealed-beam lights should shine down and to the right. On high beam, the two other headlights should flash on and light the road at a greater distance. If your car has only two headlights, both should shine with the dimmer switch in either position.

2 Turn the ignition switch to the accessory position and put the turn signal indicator arm down. The appropriate light on the dashboard should light up and click on and off. If it stays on, either the front or rear indicator bulb on that side is burned out or the connection is bad. Repeat to check the other directional signal.

3 Flip on the emergency flasher light switch located on the steering column or the dashboard. Have your helper check the front flashers first. Then in the rear of the car he can check four sets of lights (the flashers, the driving lights, the stop lights, and the backup lights).

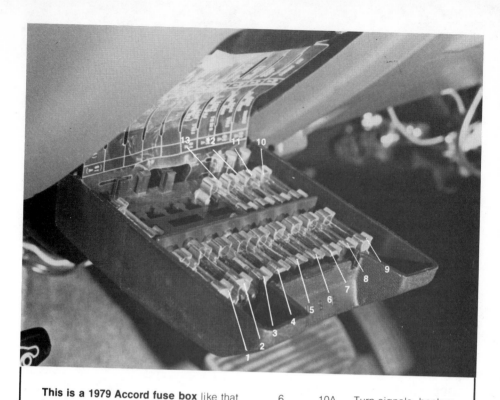

This is a 1979 Accord fuse box like that found on 1976–79 Accords, including the LX and four-door models.

CODE NO.	FUSE SIZE	MAIN COMPONENTS
1	15A	Stop light, hazard relay, horns
2	10A	Clock, cigar lighter, interior lights
3	15A	Dash lights, taillights, marker lights, license lights.
4	15A	Radio, rear window defroster
(4)	(15A)	(Low beam headlights on 1976–78)
5	20A	Heater blower
(5)	(15A)	(High-beam head lamps on 1976–78)
6	10A	Turn signals, backup lights, gauges (fuel and temperature)
7	10A	Fuel pump, voltage regulator, carburetor solenoids
8	10A	Wiper and washer, front and rear
9	10A	Right high-beam headlamp
(9)	(15A)	(Heater on 1976–78)
10	10A	Left high beam headlamp
(10)	(15A)	(Radio, rear window defroster)
11	10A	Right low-beam headlamp
12	10A	Left low-beam headlamp
13	10A	Air conditioner (if equipped)

To replace the headlight bulb

1 Remove the headlight retaining ring. There are three slotted tabs around it (some models may require the removal of the headlight trim first). To remove the retaining ring, loosen the three retaining screws, then turn the ring counterclockwise until the enlarged portion of the slots comes under the screw heads. Now remove the ring and bulb, being careful not to let the bulb slip out.

2 Pull the headlight forward and unhook the electrical connector. On Civic 1200

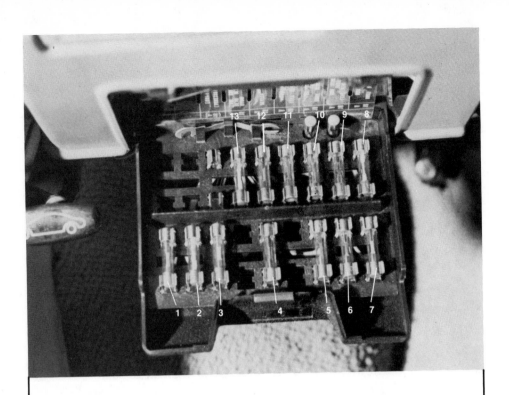

The 1979–80 Prelude and the 1980 Accord models including the LX and four-door share a similar fuse panel.

CODE NO.	FUSE SIZE	MAIN COMPONENTS
1	15A	Stop lights, hazard relay, horns
2	10A	Clock, cigar lighter, interior lights
3	15A	Dash lights, taillights, marker lights, license light.
4	15A	Engine cooling fan, air conditioner (if so equipped)
5	10A	Turn signals, backup lights, gauges (fuel and temperature)
6	10A	Fuel pump, voltage regulator, carburetor solenoids
7	15A	Wiper and washer, front and rear (if so equipped)
8	10A	Right high-beam headlamp
9	10A	Left high-beam headlamp
10	10A	Right low-beam headlamp
11	10A	Left low-beam head lamp
12	15A	Heater blower
13	15A	Radio, rear window defroster
14	10A	Air conditioner (if so equipped)

sedans and CVCC sedans and wagons, the electrical connector may be disconnected first from the engine compartment.

3 Install the new headlight by attaching the wire connector. On models with a two-headlight system, make sure you install a No. 2 light. On Accord models with a four-

The 1980 Civic sedan and wagon have a new style fuse panel.

CODE NO.	FUSE SIZE	MAIN COMPONENTS
1	15A	Wiper and washer, front and rear (if so equipped)
2	10A	Fuel pump, voltage regulator, carburetor solenoids
3	10A	Turn signals, backup lights, gauges (fuel and temperature)
4	15A	Engine cooling fan, air conditioner (if so equipped)
5	15A	Heat blower
6	15A	Radio, rear window defroster
7	15A	Stop lights, hazard relay, horns
8	10A	Clock, cigar lighter, interior lights
9	15A	Dash lights, taillights, marker lights, license light
10	10A	Left high-beam headlamp
11	10A	Right high-beam headlamp
12	10A	Left low-beam headlamp
13	10A	Right low-beam headlamp

headlight system, the No. 2 light goes on the outboard side and a No. 1 light goes on the inboard side.

4 Place the headlight bulb in position by aligning the tabs on the back of the bulb with the indentations in the mounting ring. Now reinstall the retaining ring with the enlarged portion of the slotted holes over the retaining screw heads. Turn the ring clockwise and tighten the screws.

5 Check the headlights on both high and low beam to make sure they are operating properly. Install the headlight trim if it was removed, and have the headlight adjustment checked.

To replace rear stop, turn signal, and parking light bulbs

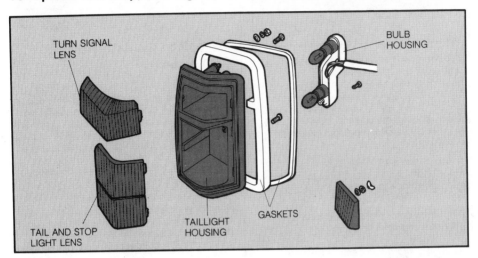

TURN SIGNAL LENS

BULB HOUSING

TAIL AND STOP LIGHT LENS

TAILLIGHT HOUSING

GASKETS

This is an exploded view of the rear taillight assembly on the 1977 CVCC sedan. To replace stop, turn signal, and parking light bulbs, the bulb housing (held in by two self-tapping screws) must be removed from inside the car through an access hole on 1973–79 Civic 1200s and 1975–79 CVCC sedans and wagons. On Accords and LX models, the inside rear panel must be removed to gain access to these bulbs. On the Prelude and four-door models, a plastic covering must be removed from the light assemblies from inside the trunk compartment.

1 Remove the bad bulb.

2 Install the new bulb by aligning the pins on the base of the bulb with the proper slot in the socket. The locating pins on the base of double filament bulbs are staggered to prevent incorrect installation. Install the bulb into the socket and turn it clockwise to lock it in place.

3 If the bulb does not turn, it is incorrectly aligned. Remove it, turn it one-half a turn, and reinstall it.

To replace backup, side marker, front turn, and parking light bulbs

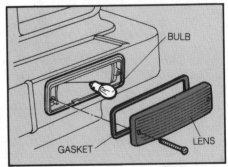

BULB

GASKET

LENS

1 Remove the retaining screws, which are visible from outside the car, from the lens of the malfunctioning bulb. Now remove the lens and the faulty bulb can be removed.

2 Install a new bulb and align the pins on the base with the proper slot in the socket. Replace the gasket (if removed), lens, and retaining screws.

To replace the license plate lights

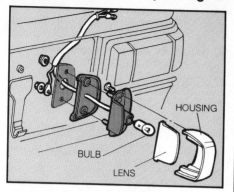

HOUSING

BULB

LENS

1 To replace the license plate bulb on all models (except 1979–80 Preludes and 1980 Civics), you must remove the light housing assembly first. To remove the housing, the inner trim panel has to be removed, then the two nuts holding the housing assembly. Now the assembly can be separated by removing the two retaining screws.

OR if you own a 1979–80 Prelude or 1980 Civic, the lens may be taken out by removing the two retaining screws from the outside and removing the lens, thus exposing the bulb.

2 On all models, remove the bulb by gently pushing on it and turning counterclockwise.
CAUTION: Some bulbs become stuck or corroded in the socket after a long time. It is safer when replacing any bulb to wrap it in a rag, just in case it breaks, but this is especially important when replacing old bulbs.

3 Install the new bulb by pushing in on it and rotating it clockwise. Replace the lens with the two retaining screws on Preludes and 1980 Civics. On other models, reassemble the housing, then reinstall it back onto the car and replace the inner trim panel.

To replace the dash warning light bulbs

The dash warning light bulbs are only accessible through the access panel on 1980 Civics. This rectangular panel is in the top of the dash above the instrument gauges. On these models, pry the access panel up to expose the bulb. The bulb can be removed by turning it counterclockwise. Reinstall the new bulb and then the access panel.

Replacing other dash light bulbs on the 1980 Civic as well as all dash light bulbs on all other models requires the removal of the instrument cluster. This should be left to a professional mechanic.

Bulb data

BULB REPLACEMENT CHART								
	1980 CIVIC		CIVIC 1200 CIVIC SEDAN CVCC WAGON		ACCORD		PRELUDE	
Item	CP/W	SAE#	CP/W	SAE#	CP/W	SAE#	CP/W	SAE#
Headlamp								
outer (or single)	60/50W	6014	60/50W	6014	38/50W	4002	65/55W	6052
inner					38W	4001		
Front lamps								
turn signal/parking	32/3CP	1157	32/3CP	1157	32/3CP	1157	32/3CP	1157
Rear lamps								
stop/tail	32/3CP	1157	32/3CP	1157	32/3CP	1157	32/3CP	1157
turn signal	32CP	1156	32CP	1156	32CP	1156	32CP	1156
backup	32CP	1156	32CP	1156	32CP	1156	32CP	1156
Side marker	2CP	194	4CP	67	2CP	194	2CP	194
License	4CP	67	4CP	67	4CP	67	4CP	67
Interior	5W	N/A	5W	N/A	8W	N/A	5W	N/A
Hatch or trunk	3.4W	N/A	5W	N/A	5W	N/A	5W	N/A

* CP—Candle power, W—Wattage, SAE#—Trade number

To replace dome, hatch, and trunk lights

1 The lenses on the dome, hatch, and trunk lights can be squeezed on the sides (even the round lenses) and snapped out. It is not necessary to take the entire assembly out, but if it does come out, you can easily snap it back into place.

2 To remove the bulb, which is cylindrical and resembles a fuse with points on the end, gently hold the clip back and lift the bulb out. To install a new bulb, position it on the clips and press it into place.

Replace light, dimmer, and turn-signal switches

On 1975–80 Hondas, the light switch, dimmer switch, and turn-signal switch are all part of a single combination switch. On 1973–74 Hondas, only the turn signal and dimmer switch are on a combination switch. The switches are located on the steering column below the steering wheel. If any of these switches are diagnosed as faulty, you may replace the combination switch.

1 Disconnect the battery.

2 Remove the steering wheel by pulling the center steering wheel pad off on 1973–79 Civic 1200s, 1975–79 CVCC sedans and wagons, and 1976–80 Accords. On Preludes and 1980 Civics, pry the center emblem.

3 Remove the center steering wheel nut (use a 17mm socket on most models).

4 Mark the steering wheel to the steering shaft splines with a grease pencil or a light crayon.

5 Remove the steering wheel by tapping from underneath with a rubber mallet if necessary.

6 Remove the turn signal cancelling sleeve.

7 Remove the lower steering column cover by removing the five screws from underneath.

8 Loosen (but do not remove) the lock screw in the lower portion of the switch. It may be necessary to move the turn-signal switch up to loosen this screw.

9 Follow the switch wire harness to about the midpoint of the steering column and disconnect the electrical snap connector.

10 Lift the switch off and remove the windshield washer/wiper switch carefully if it is to be reused.

11 Install the new combination switch assembly by reversing the above removal procedure.

To replace the ignition switch

If diagnosis indicates a faulty ignition switch, the replacement is not difficult, but may be a little time consuming for the novice. This removal procedure is the same on all Hondas.

1 Remove the five screws (on most models) **holding the lower steering column cover** and separate it from the upper cover.

2 Locate the shear bolts, center punch and drill out each bolt using a ¼-inch drill.

3 Remove the ignition switch and disconnect the electrical connector.

4 Install the new ignition switch on the steering column, but do not tighten it yet.

5 Use the ignition key to make sure the ignition switch steering lock operates properly.

6 Tighten the shear bolts. The bolt heads should twist off.

7 Reconnect the electrical connector and install the lower steering column cover.

Replace the windshield wiper blades

If your windshield wipers are smearing the glass, chances are the wiper blades should be replaced. The rubber part has most likely become hard and damaged by wiping over accumulated dirt on the windshield. It is also likely that the wiper arms have lost tension and therefore do not apply enough pressure on the blades to wipe the glass clean. Replacing the wiper blades only takes a few minutes and you can do it yourself.

1 To remove the wiper blade, front or rear, locate the blade lock, move the tab to unlock it, and pull the blade off the end of the wiper arm.

2 To install a new wiper blade, lift the wiper arm clear from the windshield and slide on the new blade until the tab clicks firmly into place.

Flatblade and Phillips-head screwdrivers

Ratchet, sockets, handles, and universal joint

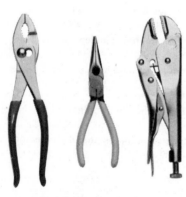

Slip-joint, long-nose, and locking-jaw pliers

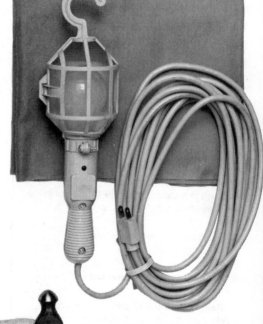

Adjustable wrench

Ball-peen hammer

Droplight and fender cover

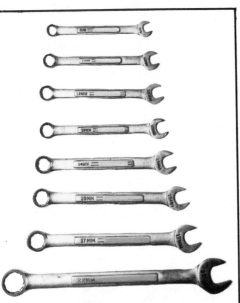

Combination box- and open-end wrenches

Basic Tools

Check your toolbox and compare its contents with the tools shown at the left. If you're missing any, fill in those you don't have before starting to work on your car.

You'll probably want to buy the least expensive tools that will effectively do the job. The very cheapest tool is almost always inadequate. And the very best is superadequate for your purposes. Your best bet is the moderately priced tool. Let's run down the list of basic tools:

Screwdrivers. You'll need at least three flatblade types—small, medium, and large, and a stubby screwdriver helps you work in tight places. You can get by with two Phillips-heads—a #2 and a stubby one.

Pliers. Your toolbox should have at least three: a 6- to 8-inch long slip-joint steel pliers; long-nose pliers about six inches long; and a pair of locking-jaw pliers.

Adjustable wrench. One's enough. Use it when you can't carry a complete set of fixed-opening wrenches with you or for turning nuts and bolts of odd sizes.

Ratchet wrenches and sockets. Actually you'll need only one or two ratchet handles to turn your many sockets. Sockets come in standard depths for most nuts and deep sizes for removing spark plugs and nuts that have a lot of bolt sticking out from them. A universal socket is handy when a bolt or nut is difficult to reach.

Combination wrenches. One end is a box wrench, the other an open-end wrench. With a box wrench, you can apply more torque to a tight nut or bolt without the risk of the wrench slipping off. An open-end wrench, however, slips easily over a nut or bolt. It pays to buy a complete set.

Ball-peen hammer. This is the basic hammer for auto mechanics. Get a good one with a 8-, 12-, or 16-ounce head.

Droplight. You'll need either a standard droplight (shown) or one of the newer fluorescent tubes, which are more expensive but safer.

Fender cover. It's expensive, but useful. If you don't want to spend the money for the professional type, use an old shower curtain, blanket or beach towel.

Oil changing gear. You'll need a drain pan (get one large enough to hold all your car's oil and then some), an oil filter wrench, a flexible-neck funnel (for transmission fluid), and a combination opener and pour spout.

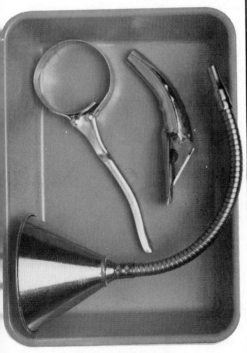

Oil changing gear

Appendix

Lubrication

NUMBER	LUBRICATION POINTS		LUBRICANT
1	Engine		API Service Grade: SE SAE Viscosity: See chart below
2	Transmission	Manual Transmission Hondamatic	SAE 10W–30 or 10W–40 SE grade oil Automatic Transmission Fluid (types A to D)
3	Brake		Brake Fluid DOT 3 or DOT 4
4	Front wheel bearings and seals*		Multipurpose Grease
5	Rear wheel bearings and seals*		
6	Tie-rod ball joints*		
7	Suspension ball joints*		
8	Steering gearbox (when disassembled) and rack		
9	Shift-lever ball*		
10	Steering-wheel horn contact*		
11	Steering-column bushings*		
12	Pedal linkage*		
13	Brake master-cylinder push-rod clevis pin*		
14	Door hinges (upper)		
15	Door hinges (lower)		
16	Door-opening detents		
17	Hood latch		
18	Hood hinges		
19	Battery bracket nuts		
20	Battery terminals (two places)		
21	Rear brake shoe linkage*		
22	Front shock absorber bearings		
23	Parking-brake-cable pivot point		
24	Caliper*	Piston seal Dust seal (boot)	Silicone Grease
25	Constant velocity joints		Molybdenum disulfide grease
26	Power steering reservoir (where so equipped)		Honda Power-steering Fluid

* These very difficult lube jobs are better left to a pro.

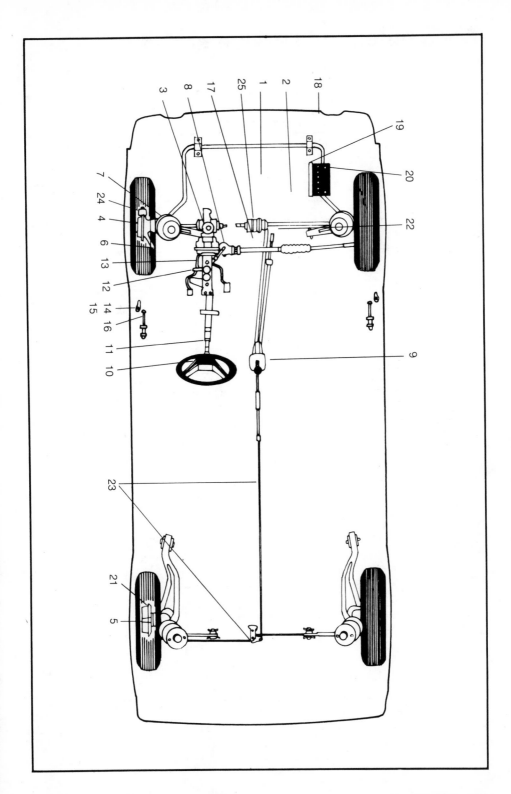

Recommended service schedules

I—Inspect   **C—Clean**   **R—Replace**

SERVICE	RECOMMENDED INTERVALS (× 1000 MILES)								NOTES
	7.5	15	22.5	30	37.5	45	52.5	60	
Engine oil	R	R	R	R	R	R	R	R	3.0ℓ (3.2 qts.) w/filter change (SAE 10W–40)
Oil filter	R	R	R	R	R	R	R	R	
Manual transmission 4-SP				R				R	2.5ℓ (2.6 qts.) (SAE 10W–40)
5-SP				R				R	2.7ℓ (2.8 qts.) (SAE 10W–40)
Hondamatic fluid		R				R			2.5ℓ (2.6 qts.) DEXRON® A.T.F
Rear brake			I					I	Minimum thickness: 2 mm (0.08 in.)
Parking brake	I								Fully engaged: 4–8 clicks
Rear wheel bearing grease								R	Use multi-purpose grease
Front brake pad and rotor		I		I		I		I	Min. thickness: Pad (lining) 1.6 mm (0.06 in.) Rotor 9.0 mm (0.35 in.)
Suspension mounting bolts	I	I		I		I		I	Check tightness of bolts
Exhaust pipe & muffler	I	I		I		I		I	Check condition and tightness
Fuel hose								R	Check for leaks and deteriorated hoses
Steering box & Tie Rods	I			I				I	Check rack grease, and steering linkage. To adjust rack guide screw: Back off 45° ± 15° from bottomed.
Brake hoses, lines & fluid	I	I		I		I		I	
Brake fluid				R				R	Use only DOT 3 or 4 fluid
Clutch release arm	I	I	I	I	I	I	I	I	Free play at arm: 3–4 mm (1/8–5/32 in.)
Cooling system hoses & connections				I				I	
Coolant				R				R	Cooling system capacity 1300: 5.0ℓ (1.32 U.S. gals.) 1500: 6.0ℓ (1.58 U.S. gals) Check specific gravity for freezing point
Alternator belt			I					I	12–17 mm (0.5–0.7 in.) @ 9–11 kg (20–24 lbs.) tension.
Distributor cap & rotor								I	
Ignition wiring								I	Maximum resistance 25,000 ohms

Tune-up specifications

Year	Model	Spark Plug			Ignition			
		Type	Gap, In.	Breaker Gap In.	Dwell Angle Deg.	Firing Order	Timing & Mark Location
1973–74	Civic	B6ES[1]	.030	.020	49–55	1342	[2]
1975	Civic CVCC	B6ES[1]	.030	.020	49–55	1342	[3][4]
	Civic	BP6ES	.030	.020	49–55	1342	7°BTDC[5]
1976	Civic CVCC	B6ES[6]	.030	.020	49–55	1342	[3][7]
	Civic	—	.030	.020	49–55	1342	7°BTDC[5]
	Accord	B6ES[6]	.030	.020	49–55	1342	[3][9]
1977	Civic CVCC	B6ES[10]	.030	.020	49–55	1342	[3][11]
	Accord	B6EB[10]	.030	.020	49–55	1342	[3][13]
1978	Civic 1200	—	.030	.020	49–55	1342	2°BTDC[3]
	Civic CVCC	B6EB[10]	.030	.020	49–55	1342	[3][14]
	Accord	B6EB[10]	.030	.020	49–55	1342	[3][14]
1979	Civic 1200	[17]	.030	.020	49–55	1342	2°BTDC[3]
	Civic CVCC	[18]	.030	.020	49–55	1342	[3][14]
	Accord[19]	B7EB	.030	—	—	1342	[3][20]
	Accord[22]	B7EB	.030	—	—	1342	[3][23]
1980	Civic 1300	W20ES-L11[24]	.041	—	—	1342	2°BTDC[3]
	Civic 1500	B7EB-11[25]	.041	—	—	1342	[3][26]
	Accord	[27]	[26]	—	—	1342	[3][28]
	Prelude	[27]	[27]	—	—	1342	TDC[3]

[1]—Under conditions of continuous low speed operation, 30 mph or lower use B5ES.

[2]—With idle retard disonnected, 5° BTDC; with idle retard connected, TDC.

[3]—Man. trans., TDC; auto. trans., 3°ATDC.

[4]—Mark located on flywheel.

[5]—Mark located on pulley.

[6]—For extended high speed driving, use B7ES.

[7]—All man. trans. models & sedan w/auto. trans., 2°BTDC; sta. wag. w/auto. trans., TDC.

[8]—Sta. wag. +1°; all others, +1¾°.

[9]—Man. trans., 2°BTDC; auto. trans., TDC.

[10]—For extended high speed driving, use B7EB.

[11]—Except Calif. & high altitude, 6°BTDC; California, except sta. wag. w/auto. trans. 2°BTDC, sta. wag. w/auto. trans. TDC; high altitude, man. trans. 2°BTDC, auto. trans. TDC.

[13]—Except Calif., man. trans. 2°BTDC, auto. trans. TDC; California, 6°BTDC.

[14]—Except Calif. & high altitude, 6°BTDC; California & high altitude, 2°BTDC

[17]—Standard, Nippon Denso, W20EP; for extended high speed driving, use W22EP.

[18]—Except Calif., Nippon Denso W20ES-L; California, NGK B6EB.

[19]—Except Calif. & high altitude.

[20]—Man. trans., 6°BTDC; auto trans., 4°BTDC.

[21]—Includes filter.

[22]—California & high altitude.

[23]—Man. trans., TDC; auto. trans., 2°ATDC.

[24]—Nippon Denso.

[25]—NGK.

[26]—Auto. trans. all & Calif. & high altitude man. trans., TDC; man. trans. except Calif. & high altitude, hatchback 15°BTDC, sta. wag. 10°BTDC.

[27]—Except Calif., B7EB gapped at .030"; California, B7EB-11 gapped at .041".

[28]—Except Calif. sedan w/5 spd. man. trans., TDC; California sedan w/5 spd. man. trans., 4°ATDC.

Index